THE WRITER IN THE GARDEN

The **WRITER** *in*

the GARDEN

edited by

JANE GARMEY

ALGONQUIN BOOKS OF CHAPEL HILL 1999

Published by
ALGONQUIN BOOKS OF CHAPEL HILL
Post Office Box 2225
Chapel Hill, North Carolina 27515-2225

a division of
WORKMAN PUBLISHING
708 Broadway
New York, New York 10003

For permission to reprint essays and poems in this volume, grateful acknowl-
edgment is made to the holders of copyright, publishers, or representatives
named on pages 247–50, which constitute an extension of the copyright page.

Library of Congress Cataloging-in-Publication Data
The writer in the garden / edited by Jane Garmey.
          p.   cm.
     ISBN 1-56512-181-3
     1. Gardens—Literary collections.   2. Gardening—Literary
  collections.   I. Garmey, Jane.
  PN6071.G27W75   1999
  810.8'0364—dc21   98–41045
                                                                CIP

10   9   8   7   6   5   4   3   2   1
First Edition

CONTENTS

CONTENTS

DESIGN IN THE GARDEN

CONTENTS

SEASONS IN THE GARDEN

THE BOUNTY
OF THE GARDEN

GARDEN VARIETY

INTRODUCTION

It's amazing how much time one can spend in a garden doing nothing at all. I sometimes think, in fact, that the nicest part of gardening is walking around in a daze, idly deadheading the odd dahlia, wondering where on earth to squeeze in yet another impulse buy, debating whether to move the recalcitrant artemisia one more time, or daydreaming about where to put the pergola. Of course, gardening is time-consuming, repetitive, and, at times, quite discouraging. But precisely because making a garden means constantly making choices, it offers almost limitless possibilities for surprise and satisfaction.

The same is true for books on gardening. They offer all kinds of choices. And the best of them are those in which the writers are willing to share their own experiences as well as admitting to their occasional moments of failure. With disarming generosity, they invite us into their gardens, anguish with us over seemingly insurmountable problems, take us along on philosophical excursions, reveal strange enthusiasms, draw frequently on the past, and speculate on future plans. In other words, they are not *just* writers, they are practitioners.

A garden writer does not, of course, have to have produced a Sissinghurst, but there is no substitute for having spent two months coaxing a reluctant camellia into bloom. As readers, we don't demand encyclopedic knowledge and may yawn at didactic writing. However, we do look for the discernment that comes from hands-on experience and crave the opinions of those who still have traces of dirt on their hands. We don't at all object to partiality but prefer it braced with intelligence and wit. We love sensual details and quirky perspectives. Most of all, we enjoy a discursive tone and the kind of intuition that results from having "been there."

That authority is wonderfully epitomized by the following admonition, administered so gently and firmly by Vita Sackville-West to one of her more curmudgeonly readers:

> May I assure the gentleman who writes to me (quite often) from a priory in Sussex that I am not the armchair, library-fireside gardener he evidently suspects, "never having performed any single act of gardening" myself, and that for the last forty years of my life I have broken my back, my fingernails, and sometimes my heart, in the practical pursuit of my favorite occupation.

Curiously enough I've found that most people don't read garden books from cover to cover, even those of a writer as celebrated as Vita Sackville-West. Here is an author whose writing style is lively, sophisticated, at times engagingly diffident. And if this weren't enough, who has not heard of that extraordinary garden and that unusual life she led when not writing her columns or tending her garden? Yet, even *her* books are best read piecemeal— dipped into at random, a chapter at a time in no particular order, to be enjoyed, put aside, and come back to later.

This way of reading is not undisciplined, although I confess to having once thought it must reveal a character flaw in me, if not some undiagnosed learning disability. I occasionally used to make an effort to mend my ways, but it never made any difference. Then I discovered that others felt the same, that we had each found for ourselves the way garden books were meant to be read—a small discovery but liberating. In thinking more about this phenomenon, I've come to realize that since tastes and obsessions in one's own gardening life fluctuate from season to season, it stands to reason that hardly anyone wants to read *everything* a particular author has to say about his gardening experiences all at once. But, of course, when we find ourselves, without any warning, who knows why, absolutely smitten by hellebores (a plant genus we'd never paid much attention to before), we rush to pull down from the bookshelf our favorite books, those whose authors have taken on the roles of trusted friends and mentors. We must know what Eleanor Perényi thinks about these plants and there's a special kind of satisfaction in finding out the very spot where Gertrude Jekyll liked to have them in her garden.

Since nothing ever really gets finished in a garden and everything is always in a state of flux, it is usually the process itself that fascinates. For this reason, the best garden writing tends not to be the practical, how-to category of garden book but the work of writers who are meditative and non-prescriptive. Many garden books, in fact, consist of pieces written over a period of time. It is, therefore, a genre of writing particularly well-suited to being anthologized. An anthology becomes a way of extending and prolonging the "conversation" that runs through any good book of garden writing, allowing the reader to experience several different points of view, to pick up nuance, and even to see genuine disagreement about a topic.

This book began by way of an audio anthology I assembled called *The Writer in the Garden*. The inspiration for that venture came from once seeing a gardener wearing earphones while weeding. It made me think how pleasant it would be to listen to

Henry Mitchell as I grappled with some of those less than thrilling garden chores, how invigorating to plant bulbs in the company of Allen Lacy or Louise Beebe Wilder, and what fun to drive off to the nursery in search of an all elusive *Verbena bonariensis* while at the same time receiving some practical advice from Elizabeth Lawrence.

I've now had the luxury of expanding the audio anthology into an actual book. The word *luxury* is not an exaggeration. In search of additional material, I've had the pleasure of going back to the work of many writers I love, as well as discovering new ones. Some of these authors are rightly considered classics in the field. Others are recognized writers but not known primarily for their garden writing. Still others, from both sides of the Atlantic, are newer writers whose work I am particularly pleased to be including in this book. What all of them have in common is a distinctive voice. It is this more than anything else that has guided my choices.

Hearing these voices and being part of the conversation that has gone on in my head for the last year has led to a recurring fantasy. I am invited to a party—held, of course, in a spectacular garden. There I get to meet all the writers whose work is represented in this book. First I come upon Michael Pollan and James Schuyler, who are intently discussing whether the more subtle charms of 'Souvenir de la Malmaison' can measure up to the flagrant sexuality of 'Madame Hardy'. Eleanor Perényi is deep in conversation with Russell Page. Stephen Lacey can be seen in the distance enthusiastically defending a somewhat unorthodox planting scheme to Christopher Lloyd, while Richardson Wright and Sara Stein are comparing notes on weeds. Geoffrey Charlesworth is showing off his latest horticultural find to an admiring Beverley Nichols, who has just finished recounting one of his cat's latest foibles to Gertrude Jekyll. She is charmed but must hurry over to have a quick word with Patti Hagan before having to leave.

Katharine White, the most elegantly dressed woman present, is in search of Jamaica Kincaid, while E. B. White has bent over to finger the mulch around a particularly rare young viburnum. W. S. Merwin has been wanting to meet Mirabel Osler for years, and they are now inseparable. Robert Dash, done in by a day's work of transplanting four, or was it forty, huge flats of seedling leeks, graciously pours a drink for Thalassa Cruso, who is clearly amused by one of his outrageous stories. Then, all eyes turn to the gate, through which Edith Wharton is about to make an entrance. Conversation is hushed, but only for a moment.

Alas, like Eleanor Perényi's favorite gardener, this party never existed. But here they all are, this delicious group of garden writers, if not in person then at least between the covers of a single book. The original Greek meaning of the word *anthology* is a collection or gathering of flowers in bloom. How perfectly appropriate. What more is there to say other than please read on. Pick and peruse, haphazardly, of course. Dawdle and linger, taking as much time as you want, and put together a bouquet of your own making.

—J. G.

THE WRITER IN THE GARDEN

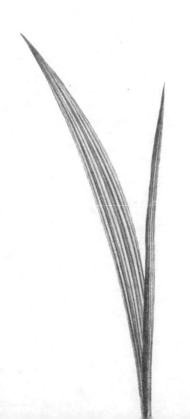

A TASTE FOR GARDENS

Half the interest of a garden is the constant
exercise of the imagination. You are always
living three, or indeed six, months hence.
I believe that people entirely devoid of imagination never can be really good gardeners. To be content with the present, and not
striving about the future, is fatal.

—*ALICE MORSE EARLE, 1897*

A Garden Like a Life

BY JANICE EMILY BOWERS

A garden, like a life, is composed of moments. I wish mine could always be as it is right now, this late afternoon at the end of March. Sunlight washes the upper branches of the mesquite tree. Orange cups of California poppy have closed for the day; white ones of evening primrose are about to open. Pink, white, lavender, purple, and cerise sweet peas quiver like butterflies tethered to a trellis. Wands of red-flowered penstemon bend under the probing of an Anna's hummingbird. Plump, black carpenter bees, shiny as patent leather shoes, steer toward the grapefruit tree, now a mass of stiff, white flowers. A breeze intermittently removes its fragrance, but between gusts the scent of my childhood drifts across the yard to me.

The first garden I remember, my paternal grandmother's, smelled like citrus blossoms, too. It seems that I can recall her garden in every detail until I try to grasp it. Then it fades into tantalizing shapes and colors and the hugeness of the spaces that a child sees. Mostly I remember row upon row of flowers, an immense expanse of blossoms it seemed then—dahlias, cosmos, roses, stocks, marigolds, marguerites, hollyhocks, phlox. I was afraid to walk among them because of the bees, and my heavy, slow-moving grandmother seemed a paragon of bravery as she stooped to pull weeds and cut deadheads. At the very back of the garden a row of sprawling blackberry vines exacted their tribute of blood in exchange for fruit. As I stood at the vines and looked back across the flowers and paths, the house seemed so far away I could conceivably get lost on the return trip.

Now I would love to be lost in such a garden. Mine is too small for that, though, so I lose myself in its moments instead. Seeing my garden as it is right now, I remember other moments at other times of year: the winter garden's tidy rows of broccoli, carrots, leeks, and beets; the summer garden's sprawling tomatoes and rambunctious melon vines. And I anticipate moments yet to come: when the first ripe tomato fills my mouth with the flavors of Italy and summertime, or when the mammoth sunflowers, now scrunched tightly like bunched paper bags, expand into upturned faces. Even though there's hardly a square centimeter of space left unplanted, I yearn to create as many moments as possible, to cram my garden to capacity or beyond, and I often stop by the nursery to thumb through the seed racks. Where in the world are you going to plant them? I ask myself every time my fingers close around a packet. Eventually, I escape with only one or two—golden zucchini for a fourth hill of squash, say, and purple beans for, well, someplace.

At the beginning, when my garden was new and thoughts of it agitated my days and dreams, I kept inviting friends to come and see my backyard paradise. They'd stroll the gravel paths, duly appreciative of the flowers and vegetables but never, it seemed to me, enthusiastic enough. Was this because my garden was actually rather dull? Or were they blind to its true beauty and real fascination? Finally, I realized that what makes my garden exciting is me. Living in it every day, participating minutely in each small event, I see with doubled and redoubled vision. Where friends notice a solitary hummingbird pricking the salvia flowers, I recall a season's worth of hummingbird battles. Where they see an ordinary mockingbird, I know a distinct individual whom I've studied as a forager, fighter, and performer. My friends, present in the garden only transiently, notice the surface prettiness, admire, and pass on to matters of more substance, while I see not merely the garden at this particular moment, but the garden as it has been at all other moments and as it will be in moments yet to come.

It astounds me still that I can succeed at gardening, as though the growing of food and flowers should be so arcane that only an alchemist could carry it off. "Of course, I won't be very good at gardening. My garden won't look nice. It won't produce well." Those ideas were firmly in place at the beginning, and it's startling to find they're not true.

Even though I've been a professional botanist for more than a decade, I never intended to have a garden. For years, in fact, I was content with my quixotic image as a botanist who couldn't grow plants, and when friends, hoping for a diagnosis, described their yellowing philodendrons or spotted ficus benjaminas, I would shrug apologetically and say, "I'm not that kind of botanist." Wild plants were my passion, and I took more interest in the weeds at the curb than in the bed of chrysanthemums three feet away. But wherever passion exists, the energy for transformation exists, too, and it was almost inevitable that I'd eventually become a gardener.

Or perhaps my garden represents less the imperatives of fate than the workings of mere chronology, which, like biology, can sometimes be destiny. As a friend of a friend ambiguously replied when asked if she gardened, "If you can call it that. Forty is about the age for that sort of thing, isn't it?" She was right. Forty is about the age for unexpected developments: extroverts turn introspective, introverts become sociable, and everyone, without regard to type, acquires gray hairs and philosophies of life. Many also acquire gardens.

If I close my eyes, I can remember what this space looked like before: a stubble of dead bermuda grass on parched earth, patches of weeds according to season, a sunburned hedge on one side of the yard, stumps of dead grapevine on the other. All it needed to complete the picture was a broken-down car on blocks. I was not unwilling for this state of affairs to continue indefinitely, and, one day, when without a word of preamble or explanation, my husband outlined a flower bed on the stubbled dirt, the main question in my mind was, "How in the world are we going to fill that enormous space?" A garden seemed as unlikely as a Tasmanian devil, and all my husband's grubbing out of moribund shrubbery and laying of drip-irrigation lines represented nothing more than the great masculine tradition of yard work. Certainly it held no potential interest for me. After all, I wasn't that kind of botanist.

But I couldn't very well sit indoors reading a book while he labored alone with shovel, wheelbarrow, hoe, and rake. Human courtesy (not to mention matrimonial harmony) demanded that I assist. Just as the throwing of a stick triggers a retriever's fetching instinct, so the sinking of a spade into dirt released some native instinct in me. By the time the bed was dug, the drip lines laid, the paths graveled, I had graduated from assistant to partner. My husband, who knows a chronological imperative when he sees one, stepped aside at that point, and by the time the earth was fertilized and the first rows planted, I had become both head gardener and chief assistant, too. And I stuck with it. That still amazes me. I stayed with my garden.

By all previous indications, I should have been a temporary gardener, one of those for whom gardening is nothing more than another way of filling time, like painting ceramic figurines or arranging artificial flowers. But we don't give up on the things we are meant to do, which is another way of saying that the passion we bring to our activities won't allow us to quit them. What made me stick with my garden was not so much the digging (although I loved the crumble of clods between my fingers) or the produce (although I valued every single tomato, pea, green bean, and cantaloupe) or even the multiplicity of living creatures drawn by the miniature world I'd half created, half evoked. The reason I stayed in gardening was all of these combined, especially their unfolding as unexpectedly as the twists and turns of a life.

When I was a child, I would lie in bed at night and imagine all the rooms of the house in place around me: the living room just behind my head, the coat closet behind my bookshelf, the hallway to my right, my sister's room beyond my toes: every space in its exact and somewhat mysterious relation to every other space, the walls opaque to the eye but penetrable by the imagination, the whole forming a three-dimensional blueprint that represented the known and the unknown, the security of home and the possibility of explorations beyond its familiar perimeter.

In much the same way I now like to imagine my garden in its place in the neighborhood, the city, the surrounding desert. The centermost of these concentric rings is my backyard, a rectangle some eighty feet long and half as wide, bounded on one side by an unkempt pyracantha hedge and a tall board fence, on the other by a chain-link fence loosely embroidered with vines. The far end terminates at a spreading mesquite tree that volunteered long ago in the weedy alley, and the near end stops at my back door. Beyond these boundaries lie other yards, unknown except for brief glimpses from the roof or through fences, yards where swimming pools or patrolling dogs take the place of gardens, where blue morning glories riot over sunflowers and bermuda grass clutches straggling tomato plants, where potted cacti fatten on a diet of occasional water and constant sun. One after another, separated by tall hedges or block walls or wooden fences, these yards and gardens proliferate across the valley floor, each set into the grid of city streets and drainage channels, each occupying its own inviolate space yet joined by an underground network of pipes and an overhead web of wires, spilling at last onto the ragged margins of the desert. Here, where even bermuda grass hesitates and none of the cacti are in pots, we realize the utter artificiality of all that lies inside.

You'd think we could be satisfied with the desert's own peculiar beauty and abundance, especially in the rare springs when winter rains start early and countless wildflowers soften the angular slopes. Then the desert is a garden in itself. Even in the hottest, driest months, when wildflowers are a memory or a wish and an outdoor stroll is more penance than pleasure, the desert still looks something like a garden. On plains, the sparsely leaved creosote bushes space themselves as precisely as topiary in the great gardens at Versailles, and on foothills, the twiggy canopies of paloverde trees provide massed greenery in the distance. Cacti, placed just so about the landscape, could be garden statuary, especially the magnificent saguaros that poke well above the trees. A variety of indistinguishable gray shrubs would be suitable, if properly trimmed, to edge sidewalks and flower beds.

But evidently the desert itself is not garden enough. Bred to artificial climates and artificial landscapes, we want clearer distinctions and firmer boundaries for our lives.

The native vegetation here survives on ten or eleven inches of rainfall a year, part in winter, the rest in summer. Some years it makes do with much less. Then, even the saguaros, which normally contain up to a ton of water, suffer visibly as their skin shrivels between the vertical ribs until they look like half-starved dogs. We city gardeners take whatever water nature provides and add to it some thirty inches more, water withdrawn from ancient aquifers formed during wetter times. At two cents a cubic foot, water is generally the most expensive component of our gardens, and we use it as wisely as possible, even while admitting that the wisest choice would be not to use it all.

We compromise by disassembling the conventional garden into its components, tucking the parts wherever they fit: a narrow bed along the fence might hold three melon vines, a planter under the bedroom window could be an asparagus bed, the unused strip beside the house should be fine for tomatoes, and almost any place will do for the two or three eggplant bushes that more than satisfy the needs of most households. Even the lushest desert gardens show some space of bare ground since a continuous cover of green is morally indefensible as well as economically impractical.

In this way, the desert defines, determines, and delimits. The gardens that bloom so beautifully in our minds, the ones where zinnias never die of wilt and summer days are never so hot that delicate leaves turn crisp and brown, these gardens are the Platonic ideal. The gardens we're actually stuck with, the ones where green beans drop before they're the size of matchsticks, corn plants topple in thunderstorms, and summer balsam germinates but never blooms, these gardens correspond to real life. This is the garden I have made, the garden where I must live. Its virtues are my own; its faults and limitations are mine, too. It exists at my forbearance, and without my constant attention, it will die — perish all the quicker because I garden in the desert, and if a garden is an expression of personality, it is just as much an expression of place.

—from *A Full Life in a Small Place,* 1993

The Purpose of a Garden

BY SAMUEL REYNOLDS HOLE

I asked a schoolboy, in the sweet summertide, "what he thought a garden was for?" and he said, *Strawberries*. His younger sister suggested *Croquet* and the elder *Garden-parties*. The brother from Oxford made a prompt declaration in favour of *Lawn Tennis* and *Cigarettes*, but he was rebuked by a solemn senior, who wore spectacles, and more back hair than is usual with males, and was told that "a garden was designed for botanical research, and for the classification of plants." He was about to demonstrate the differences between the *Acoty-* and the *Monocoty-ledonous* divisions when the collegian remembered an engagement elsewhere.

I repeated my question to a middle-aged nymph, who wore a feathered hat of noble proportions over a loose green tunic with a silver belt, and she replied, with a rapturous disdain of the ignorance which presumed to ask—"What is a garden for? For the soul, sir, for the soul of the poet! For visions of the invisible, for grasping the intangible, for hearing the inaudible, for exaltations above the miserable dullness of common life into the splendid regions of imaginations and romance." . . . A capacious gentleman informed me that nothing in horticulture touched him so sensibly as green peas and new potatoes, and he spoke with so much cheerful candour that I could not get angry; but my indignation was roused by a morose millionaire, when he declared that of all his expenses he grudged most the outlay on his confounded garden.[. . .]

I began to fear that my intense love of a garden might be a mere hallucination, an idiosyncrasy, a want of manliness, a softening of the brain. Nevertheless I persevered in my inquiries, until I found that which I sought—the sympathy of an enthusiasm as hearty as my own, a brotherhood and a sisterhood, who, amid all the ignorance and pretence of which I have given examples, were devoted to the culture of flowers, and enjoyed from this occupation a large portion of the happiness, which is the purest and the surest we can know on earth, the happiness of Home.

—from *Our Gardens,* 1899

A Shape of Water

BY W. S. MERWIN

The garden, or what my wife and I have come to call the garden, follows a small winding valley on the north coast of the Hawaiian island of Maui. Half a mile or so beyond our property line on the seaward side the stream bed that is the keel of the valley emerges from under a thicket of pandanus trees into a grassy hollow at the top of the sea cliffs, where there was once a watercress pond, and then cuts through the edge to a series of shoulders and shelves and the rocky shoreline.

This is the rainy side of the island and in times of heavy downpours the stream bed roars and the muddy torrent can be dangerous, but most of the time there is no water in the channel at all. This part of the coast, whose name in Hawaiian means "fan," is a series of deep sinuous valleys more or less like the one where we live, opening out into basins and then narrowing again into steep gorges filled with dense growth under big trees. Some of these valleys still have their water, or a remnant of it, and the relation of the watercourses to their water is the central thread of the history of this whole area since it was first settled, and most obviously during the past two hundred years. The flow of water in the channel of massive boulders at the bottom of our garden was certainly more constant before the first irrigation ditches and tunnels were carved out of the mountainside above here over a hundred years ago, and before the serpentine coast road was cut through to Hana after the First World War. The rural life of the Hawaiians had always assumed an unfailing supply of pure water, and when the water in these valleys was cut off or severely reduced, the people who lived here, growing taro in flooded terraces surrounded by bananas and sugar cane, people whose forebears had planted the ancestors of the huge mango trees that still shade the stream bed, could no longer survive, and were forced to leave.

In the time that I have been acquainted with this region I have become increasingly aware of it as a testament of water, the origin and guide of its contours and gradients and of all the lives—the plants and small creatures, and the culture—that evolved here. That was always here to be seen, of course, and the recognition has forced itself, in one form or another, upon people in every part of the world who have been directly involved with the growing of living things. The gardener who ignores it is soon left with no garden. When Alexander Pope, that happily obsessed gardener, urged his reader, in a line that soon became famous, to "Consult the Genius of the Place in all," the primary office of that Genius as he conceived of it was to tell "the Waters or to rise, or fall." The role of water is inseparable from the character of a garden, and even its absence in a garden can take many forms. Muso Soseki, the great thirteenth-century garden designer and poet, directed water with great variety through the gardens he laid out, some of which still survive, but he was also a master of creating the suggestion of non-existent water with bare stones or steep shapes of rock, or foliage or shadows or sand, and long after his death, where moss has grown over certain of his arrangements it has continued and deepened the illusion.

When I first saw this valley and these ridges the water I was most conscious of was the sea itself, the vast expanse of brilliant moving blue stretching north to the horizon beyond which, I knew, there was no land before Alaska. Seen from the house and from the slopes of the garden now, over the leaves of heliconias and through the fronds of palms, it is the background, both visibly and in time and space, for this island is a mountain—indeed two mountains that rose from the sea and is returning to it. As long as the trades are blowing from the north and east it is above the sea that the vast ranges of clouds build up, bringing to this coast the rain that formed the valleys, made possible the forests all along the mountain, and allowed particular species of plants and insects, tiny brilliant tree snails and birds to evolve for each variation in the terrain. The rain was one of the salient attributes of the early Hawaiians' god Lono, the divinity of the growing world, who initiates each year of growth when the Pleiades, which in Hawaiian are The Little Eyes, rise above the horizon. In the poetry of the Hawaiians rain almost always is the rain of a particular place, with a specific character and an allusion to an erotic element of some story draped with names. The garden waits for the rain, responds to it at once, opens to it, holds it, takes it up and shines with it. The sound and touch and smell of the rain, the manner of its arrival, its temper and passage are like a sensuous visitation to the garden, and the light among the trees after rain, with its own depth and moment, iridescent, shifting and unseizable, is an intensified image of the garden at that instant.

But what I saw on the dry afternoon when I first picked my way down the pot-holed track toward the promontory here was the bare ridge thinly covered with long parched grass and scrub guavas thrashing in the trades, and the dust blowing. It was the end of summer and the rising notes of plovers just back from

Alaska for the winter flew in the wind. There were few buildings, and they were small and tentative in the glaring light, and there were almost no trees on the upper slopes. I did not know then that the whole coast had been a forest until some time in the last century, its principal trees the great Hawaiian *Acacia koa,* and the *'ohia* sacred to the fire goddess Pele, the maker of the islands in the first place, and the pandanus and the Hawaiian fan palm, the *loulu,* of the genus Pritchardia, which still grows in small stands in the rain forest to the east along the coast. All of this area was deforested by enterprising Caucasians, first for grazing imported cattle, then for planting sugar, to which the gradients were unsuited. After the road was hacked out above the coast a group of deluded speculators undertook to transform these slopes into a pineapple plantation. They plowed the sides of the valley vertically so that whatever topsoil had remained until then was washed away in a few years and the entrepreneurs lost their investment and left. If I had known what to look for on that first afternoon I would have been able to note the shallow parallel indentations running down through the waving grass across the valley like ripples in sand, the scars of that ruinous venture. I walked down the slope through the scrub and came to the dark green clouds of the mango trees, and under them, in the shade, caught a glimpse of another world.

Even choked, as it was then, with thickets of rampant introduced weed growth, it was the shadowy stream bed with its rocks under the huge trees that made me want to stay and so to settle, and have a garden in this valley. But also the thought of having a chance to take a piece of abused land and restoring it to some capacity of which I had only a vague idea was part of the appeal, and the day I signed the escrow papers for the land I planted, up along the ridge, the first trees of a windbreak.

From the beginning I wanted to use native species and to try growth that would have covered these sturbed. I knew it would be an arduous undertaking but it was also far more complex than I could have imagined. I did manage to find and establish a number of indigenous kinds of trees and plants, and I think that when I began I still supposed that humans could "reforest" when in fact all we can do is to plant this or that and hope that what we are doing turns out to be appropriate. Plainly I had been making my way toward such an intimation, and toward the present garden, since I was a small child in Union City, New Jersey, drawn by an inexplicable cluster of feelings, as by a magnet, to tufts of grass appearing between cracks in the stone slabs of the sidewalk. When I was nine we moved to Scranton, Pennsylvania. I thought then that I knew what a garden was. There was the one my mother made under the kitchen window along a few feet of brick walk, with portulaca, irises, larkspur, cosmos, and a red rambler on the green picket fence by the alley. And there was the Victory Garden that we made in the coal company's empty lot across the alley, after a man came at the end of winter and managed to get a horse and an old plow up over the stone curb and through the gate in the cast-iron fence and plowed up the space I knew while I watched him as though he were someone I had read about. In Europe, and in Mexico, wherever I had lived I had tended gardens with no particular skill, and had loved them, and been fed by them, but most of my questions to do with them had been practical ones, for most of were in places that had been thought of as gardens by other people, for a long time. It was here on a tropical island, on ground impoverished by human use and ravaged by a destructive history, that I found a garden that raised questions of a different kind—including what a garden really was, after all, and what I thought I was doing in it.

Obviously a garden is not the wilderness but an assembly of shapes, most of them living, that owes some share of its c position, its appearance, to human design and effort, human conventions and convenience, and the human pursuit of that elusive, indefinable harmony that we call beauty. It has a life of its own, an intricate, wilful, secret life, as any gardener knows. It is only the humans in it who think of it as a garden. But a garden is a relation, which is one of the countless reasons why it is never finished.

I have admired, and have loved gardens of many kinds, but what I aspire to, and want to have around our lives now, is a sense of the forest. It must be an illusion of the forest, clearly, for this is a garden and so a kind of fiction. But the places in the garden where I find myself lingering and staring with unsoundable pleasure are those where it looks to me as though—with the shafts of light reaching and dividing through the trees—it might be deep in the forest. Years ago I read of gardens around Taoist monasteries in the mountains of China, gardens that seemed to be the forest itself into which the mountain paths wound and the traveller discovered that the forest at every turn looked more beautiful, the perspectives and forms and the variety of greens and shadows and flowers more wonderful, and then it became apparent that the mossed stones of the path had been arranged there, and a turn brought glimpses of a low wall and bit of monastery roof appearing like a shoulder of the hillside. Behind my own fiction, I suppose, is the fond belief that something of the kind can exist.

When we have reached a point where our own kind is steadily destroying the rest of life on earth and some of us are anxious not to do that, our relation to the earth begins to be that of a gardener to a garden. I believe that gardening, the deliberate influencing of particular plants in the forest, existed for millennia before there was agriculture, and I am convinced that there was a measure of joy and magic in that relation from the beginning, something that probably sobered up considerably when it started to fall into line and become agriculture.

Such considerations turn up around me as I try to find out what the garden—this garden—may be. They raise further questions, such as the prospects for indigenous and endemic species in circumstances that have been radically altered, the particular advisability or risks of calculated or accidental introductions— plants, insects, birds, animals, including ourselves. I want a garden that is an evolving habitat in which a balance is constantly being sought and found between responsibility and provisional control.

But I certainly do not want to suggest that the garden is an earnest duty, a program of moral calisthenics undertaken like an hour at an exercise machine. If I hear the word *yardwork* I avoid the subject. For the person who has arrived at gardening at whatever age it is an enchantment, all of it, from the daydreaming to the digging, the heaving, the weeding and watching and watering, the heat, and the stirrings at the edges of the days.

Some gardens of course are communal activities, but much gardening is quiet work and a good deal of it is done alone. I have been describing my own ruminations about the garden, but my wife, Paula, and I work in it together. Part of the time on the same thing, much of the time on our own. Either way, it is what we are both doing.

Some of the things growing here now were already in the ground before we met, but it was only after it was clear that Paula wanted to live here too, after thirty years in New York, that what is around us began to be not simply an assembly of plants laboriously set into soil and conditions that had been rendered inhospitable for many of them, but a garden. Her lack of hesitation was less surprising to her than it was to me. She was born in Argentina, grew up in the tropics, and had always wanted a garden, read about gardens, imagined living in a garden. She had not been here for more than a day or two before she was out on the slope dragging long grass from around young plantings and helping to clear space for others.

Different parts of the garden have different forms. There is the food garden, a number of raised beds and a curving screen of banana trees, that supplies something or other—lemons, limes, papayas, salad, peppers, eggplant, sweet potatoes, maybe corn— for the meals of most days. But I am afraid that gets less than its share of attention regularly as a result of the allurements of grow- ing other things. Above all palms. The inaugural ambition to pro- liferate native species has endowed us with several kinds of native hibiscus, Hawaiian artemisia, trees ranging from seedlings to tall figures on the upland areas, but it came to focus on Hawaiian palms, some of them highly endangered (one, on the island of Molokai, is reduced to a single tree in the wild). Most of the species now exist in the garden, and growing them from seed led to a fascination with palms from elsewhere, and with cycads and other flora of the world's increasingly menaced tropics, and an at- tempt to make a situation where they might be able to live as though they belonged together, here in this part of this valley.

A visitor to a garden sees the successes, usually. The gar- dener remembers mistakes and losses, some for a long time, and imagines the garden in a year, and in an unimaginable future. There are young trees in the ground. The days are much too short, they go by too fast, and we wish for rain and the sound of water among the rocks.

—a shorter version of this essay was published in *House & Garden*, March 1997.

The Garden

BY ANDREW MARVELL

How vainly men themselves amaze
To win the palm, the oak, or bays,
And their incessant labours see
Crowned from some single herb, or tree,
Whose short and narrow-vergèd shade
Does prudently their toils upbraid;
While all flowers and all trees do close
To weave the garlands of repose!

Fair Quiet, have I found thee here,
And Innocence, thy sister dear?
Mistaken long, I sought you then
In busy companies of men.
Your sacred plants, if here below,
Only among the plants will grow;
Society is all but rude
To this delicious solitude.

No white nor red was ever seen
So amorous as this lovely green.
Fond lovers, cruel as their flame,
Cut in these trees their mistress' name:
Little, alas, they know or heed

How far these beauties hers exceed!
Fair trees, wheresoe'er your barks I wound,
No name shall but your own be found.

When we have run our passion's heat,
Love hither makes his best retreat.
The gods, that mortal beauty chase,
Still in a tree did end their race:
Apollo hunted Daphne so,
Only that she might laurel grow;
And Pan did after Syrinx speed,
Not as a nymph, but for a reed.

What wondrous life is this I lead!
Ripe apples drop about my head;
The luscious clusters of the vine
Upon my mouth do crush their wine;
The nectarine and curious peach
Into my hands themselves do reach;
Stumbling on melons, as I pass,
Ensnared with flowers, I fall on grass.

Meanwhile the mind from pleasure less
Withdraws into its happiness;
The mind, that ocean where each kind
Does straight its own resemblance find;
Yet it creates, transcending these,
Far other worlds and other seas,
Annihilating all that's made
To a green thought in a green shade.

Here at the fountain's sliding foot,
Or at some fruit-tree's mossy root,

Casting the body's vest aside,
My soul into the boughs does glide:
There, like a bird, it sits and sings,
Then whets and combs its silver wings,
And, till prepared for longer flight,
Waves in its plumes the various light.

Such was that happy garden-state,
While man there walked without a mate:
After a place so pure and sweet,
What other help could yet be meet!
But 'twas beyond a mortal's share
To wander solitary there:
Two paradises 'twere in one
To live in Paradise alone.

How well the skilful gardener drew,
Of flowers and herbs, this dial new;
Where, from above, the milder sun
Does through a fragrant zodiac run;
And, as it works, the industrious bee
Computes its time as well as we!
How could such sweet and wholesome hours
Be reckoned but with herbs and flowers?

—c. 1651

My Invisible Garden

BY ANNE RAVER

Sometimes my friend gives me a funny look when I talk about my garden. I was late for dinner one night because I'd lost track of the time, and I tried to explain how it is, in the garden, at twilight.

"I was mulching my potatoes . . . and wondering if marsh hay was too salty or if all those minerals from the sea would be good for them. And then I realized that I still have this fear of plants, you know, because I haven't grown potatoes before . . ."

My voice trailed off. The restaurant was noisy, and we were supposed to order quickly, because the kitchen was about to close. I thought of the wind blowing over my potato plants, now cuddled in their hay. Of the bird, with unusual black and orange markings, that had swooped low over the garden wall.

"And guess what? My cleome self-seeded."

"I think I'll have the tortellini," my friend said.

"They look like little hands," I doggedly went on. "That's how I tell them from the weeds."

She smiled, affectionately, but uncomprehendingly. The

23

funny look. The way I nod at new mothers, friends of mine, when they talk about their children. I know they're recounting something passionate, something I even want to experience, but I can't relate to the words.

Other mothers can, just as other gardeners know what happens when you start out mulching potatoes and stop to wind a pole bean around a string or notice a different bird with a strange marking or see, long after you had given up all hope, that the cleome is up.

That evening, for instance, as the light faded, and the tree branches grew black against the pink sky, I knew it was getting on toward dinnertime, but I felt so peaceful sitting like a child in the warm earth. It was dark as I strained my eyes, searching out infinitesimal parsley seedlings among the weeds.

I'd wandered by the parsley patch looking for my watering can, intending to give the potatoes a dose of sea kelp solution before going to dinner. I'd given up on the parsley, a flavorful, single-leafed Italian variety I'd direct-seeded, and figured I'd have to settle for buying some plants at my local nursery. All they sell is the curly-leafed stuff, which doesn't taste half as sweet. But as I went by, I bent over, just for a look, and there, in the twilight I spied a bit of parsley. The baby seedlings are crinkled, like teeny cupcake wrappers.

I was so happy to see them, these little jokes on my lack of faith, that I had to sit right down and pull a few weeds. Give the parsley some air and light in exchange for coming up. And it wasn't easy, because each seedling was about as big as a flea, lost in weeds as thick as a terrier's fur coat. So I slowed down a little, and paid attention to what my fingers had hold of—weed or parsley—and it got a little later, and a little later.

I'd always thought of weeding as such drudgery. And it was, in my father's garden. Work, pure and simple. Because it was his garden, his vision. It had nothing to do with mine.

But now that I have my own garden, I realize that it exists

on two planes. It grows on an earthly plane, of course, subject to the vagaries of sun and rain, the ironclad timing of sunrises and sunsets, the visitations of insects, and my own energy and moods.

But it also exists, in a more profound way, in my mind, where it has been growing for many years now. It's a complex vision of many dimensions that has little to do with the earthly garden, where plants get eaten by insects or succumb to disease or my own neglect. This garden changes every time I discover another flower or an heirloom vegetable or see an old climber rose that might want to scramble up my garden wall—even if I don't plant that flower or vegetable or rose for another ten years. It's a garden that I carry with me like a happy secret, as I go about the clamorous world outside the garden gate.

"I think I'll have the clam sauce, white," I said, closing the menu. I smiled at my friend and saw by her face that she'd had a rough day. But what I was really seeing, with my mind's eye, was the cleome. A sea of tall pink and white spidery blossoms, swaying on the evening breeze.

"So how did it go today?" I asked, thinking how, if I got up early, I'd have time to transplant the baby cleome.

It wasn't that I didn't care what my friend was saying; it's just that the garden, especially in the summer, comes in and out of the mind like a love affair. The knowledge that something's waiting for me when I get home.

"Of course she's a snob," I agreed. We were gossiping, as usual, about work. "But she is a good writer."

When could I get over to Muttontown for that aged cow manure, I was thinking. Where could I find a Carefree Beauty rose this late in the season? When was that four-inch-wide netting going to come into Hick's Nursery?

"Midweek," the man had said.

"But my limas are up already."

"Awh, a few more days isn't going to make any difference."

I worried about my limas as we ordered more wine. There was a lull in the conversation, and I started talking about my garden again.

"You've got to see these little lettuces growing all around my broccolis. And there's this perennial I don't even know the name of that somebody gave me last year, just a transplant, and now it's this wonderful huge sprawling purple thing . . . "

I stopped. Enough was enough.

It's okay, my friend said. She feels the same way about trying to take the perfect picture. Her photographer's eye has a vision that reaches beyond the realities of rain or technical snags or falling off a wall and missing the shot of a lifetime.

"I like people who are passionate about things," she said.

And when you're passionate about something, you often, mistakenly, try to get the other person to understand. You keep bringing up little details and profound events, thinking that maybe this time the person will get it, will see what you see.

And maybe she's just tried to tell you something, some inner truth, that went right over your head. This separation between people is more common than their connection.

When my friend wanders by my garden on a perfect beach day, she sees the usual state of affairs. The peas are tumbling sloppily over their fence. The parsley still needs weeding. Something has completely eaten the carrots. That gorgeous purple perennial has stopped blooming. And there I am, a mess. Sweaty and dirty, pushing a wheelbarrow back and forth. Working, it looks like.

"That's the cleome?" she says. "It looks like a weed."

I feel disappointed, for an instant, that she can't see what I see. That she doesn't have a window into my Secret Garden.

Where all the cleome is in bloom, perfect clusters of pink and white. But maybe that's good, I think, as I go about, sticking these "weeds" into place. Because a garden is like the self. It has so many layers and winding paths, real or imagined, that it can never be known, completely, even by the most intimate of friends.

—from *Deep in the Green*, 1995

Gardens of One Colour

BY VITA SACKVILLE-WEST

It is amusing to make one-colour gardens. They need not necessarily be large, and they need not necessarily be enclosed, though the enclosure of a dark hedge is, of course, ideal. Failing this, any secluded corner will do, or even a strip of border running under a wall, perhaps the wall of the house. The site chosen must depend upon the general lay-out, the size of the garden, and the opportunities offered. And if you think that one colour would be monotonous, you can have a two- or even a three-colour, provided the colours are happily married, which is sometimes easier of achievement in the vegetable than in the human world. You can have, for instance, the blues and the purples, or the yellows and the bronzes, with their attendant mauves and orange, respectively. Personal taste alone will dictate what you choose.

For my own part, I am trying to make a grey, green, and white garden. This is an experiment which I ardently hope may be successful, though I doubt it. One's best ideas seldom play up in practice to one's expectations, especially in gardening, where everything looks so well on paper and in the catalogues, but fails so lamentably in fulfilment after you have tucked your plants into the soil. Still, one hopes.

My grey, green, and white garden will have the advantage of a high yew hedge behind it, a wall along one side, a strip of box edging along another side, and a path of old brick along the fourth side. It is, in fact, nothing more than a fairly large bed, which has now been divided into halves by a short path of grey flagstones terminating in a rough wooden seat. When you sit on this seat, you will be turning your backs to the yew hedge, and from there I hope you will survey a low sea of grey clumps of foliage, pierced here and there with tall white flowers. I visualize the white trumpets of dozens of Regale lilies, grown three years ago from seed, coming up through the grey of southernwood and artemisia and cotton-lavender, with grey-and-white edging plants such as *Dianthus* 'Mrs Sinkins' and the silvery mats of *Stachys lanata,* more familiar and so much nicer under its English names of Rabbits' Ears or Saviour's Flannel. There will be white pansies, and white peonies, and white irises with their grey leaves . . . at least, I hope there will be all these things. I don't want to boast in advance about my grey, green, and white garden. It may be a terrible failure. I wanted only to suggest that such experiments are worth trying, and that you can adapt them to your own taste and your own opportunities.

All the same, I cannot help hoping that the great ghostly barn-owl will sweep silently across a pale garden, next summer, in the twilight—the pale garden that I am now planting, under the first flakes of snow.

—from *In Your Garden*, 1951

My Mother's Garden

BY PAULA DEITZ

Though I may be a city person, every summer, when the daylilies bloom along the roadsides, I yearn to have the feeling of being once more in my mother's garden near the Delaware River in Trenton, New Jersey. She has been gone almost two decades now, but I remember the day my first cousin telephoned, just before I sold the family house, to ask if she could come by to transplant the garden to her own home across the river. I agreed and was touched by this gesture but thought no more of it as I struggled to dismantle the possessions of my parents' lifetime.

Several years passed before I called on my cousin one summer afternoon and took a walk with her in the garden. I was totally unprepared for the effect of the familiar sights and smells on that typically hot, sticky afternoon along the Delaware. There, nodding in the slight breeze, were the daylilies and the hostas that had greeted me home from school for as long ago as I can remember, and the miniature box balls, now grown into a hedge, had that moist fragrance reminiscent always of old Colonial gardens. There were even a few lilac liriopes as a reminder that my mother loved purple. Set in a circle around a center of crape myrtle, the garden was not so much a memorial as a sign of continuity.

My childhood home, an earlier house in the Tudor style, was on a side street by the river, and the garden, never elaborate, remained the same each year in a progression from violets and lily-of-the-valley in spring to daylilies and borders of marigolds and ageratum in summer and mature grapevines in early autumn. I was already married when they moved to a townhouse across from the State Capitol; and though the new house remained unfamiliar, they had brought most of the garden with them. I was always happy sitting outside on my summer visits.

In many ways, my cousin, who stayed in the community I left, also developed some of my mother's interests. Now I go every summer to spend an afternoon with her in the garden where she carries on family traditions in a way I never will.

But what pleasure for me, if just for a day, to step back into time, or more properly, timelessness. On the autumn day that I sold the townhouse, I drove over to take a last look at the Tudor house. I walked straight out to the backyard, by then a bit over-grown, and there at the far end was my mother's grapevine, still going strong on the wrought-iron trellis.

Gardens never know when it is over.

—from *The Philadelphia Inquirer*, August 11, 1996

The Garden of Alcinous

BY HOMER

Close to the Gates a spacious Garden lies,
From Storms defended and inclement Skies:
Four Acres was th'allotted Space of Ground,
Fenc'd with a green Enclosure all around.
Tall thriving Trees confest the fruitful Mold;
The red'ning Apple ripens here to Gold,
Here the blue Figg with luscious Juice o'erflows,
With deeper Red the full Pomegranate glows,
The Branch here bends beneath the weighty Pear,
And verdant Olives flourish round the Year.
The balmy Spirit of the Western Gale
Eternal breathes on Fruits untaught to fail:
Each dropping Pear a following Pear supplies,
On Apples Apples, Figs on Figs arise:
The same mild Season gives the Blooms to blow,
The Buds to harden, and the Fruits to grow.

Here order'd Vines in equal Ranks appear,
With all th'United Labours of the Year.
Some to unload the fertile Branches run,
Some dry the black'ning Clusters in the Sun,
Others to tread the liquid Harvest join,

The groaning Presses foam with Floods of Wine.
Here are the Vines in early Flow'r descry'd,
Here Grapes discolour'd on the Sunny Side,
And there in *Autumn's* richest Purple dy'd.

Beds of all various Herbs, for ever green,
In beauteous Order terminate the Scene.

Two plenteous Fountains the whole Prospect crown'd;
This thro' the Gardens leads its Streams around,
Visits each Plant, and waters all the Ground:
While that in Pipes beneath the Palace flows,
And thence its Current on the town bestows;
To various Use their various Streams they bring,
The People one, and one supplies the King.

—from Homer's *Odyssey,* Book VII,
translated by Alexander Pope, 1725–26

GARDENERS IN THE GARDEN

What a man needs in gardening is a cast-iron back, with a hinge in it.

—*CHARLES DUDLEY WARNER, 1870*

Help

BY ELEANOR PERÉNYI

McC. is a Scot, a tall, lean, saturnine fellow born just short of seventy years ago near Aberdeen, and he comes from a long line of estate gardeners. The Scotch genius for horticulture has been recognized for centuries and in many countries, and McC. is a worthy successor to that tradition. He rose rapidly to the top of his profession, and after his emigration to America was head gardener to three Long Island millionaires, each sorry to part with him. I haven't quite understood how he came to pick our village for his retirement—"caught my fancy" is all he will say—and still less why he decided to give me some of his time. Boredom perhaps (he is quite rich and certainly doesn't need the money), or a touch of nostalgia. He once said my garden reminded him of home, by which, of course, he meant the cottage gardens of the villages, not the ordered splendors of the castle garden his father managed and where he grew up.

Anyway, I am grateful, because what McC. doesn't know about horticulture isn't worth bothering about. He carries a knife, curved like a crane's bill and sharpened to a deadly edge, and this he whips out to prune a dwarf fruit tree in minutes ("Mind you don't leave a stump; cut your branch right to the bone"); and a hedge clipped by McC., by hand, the top sloping inward, seems to know it has been barbered by an expert who doesn't tolerate gaps or snaggled branches. Things grow for McC., too, as if they recognized his authority. A seedling or a shrub planted by him sits there as if fixed by a nail, and you know it won't blow over or dare to wilt. He could graft if he had the opportunity—the technique of producing standard roses isn't beyond him—and could grow camellias and melons for me in winter if I had a greenhouse. (*He* has one, a small Lord & Burnham model.) He knows how to train grapevines and berry bushes and make them productive, and how to seduce a rose into covering the summer house. Finally, he is reliable. If he says he will drop by at ten o'clock, he drops by at ten o'clock, wearing an old suede jacket, his pruning knife in his pocket.

There is only one trouble with McC. He doesn't exist outside my fevered imagination.

Well-trained gardeners who like their work must live in America, but not around here and not in my price range. When I look back on the long procession of incompetents, dumbbells and eccentrics, young and old, foreign and domestic, who have worked for me, I wonder how I and the garden have survived their ministrations. I recall, for example, Mr. R., a well-known figure in town because in spite of his shabby get-up he is said to be very rich, with large plantations in Brazil—or it may be the Cape Verde Islands. You see him moving at a rapid hobble along the street, on his way to some garden or other, usually belonging to a newcomer because we old-timers know that he brings death and destruction with him. Those he has worked for discuss him with tears in their eyes. The summer he gardened for me he killed two cherry trees, uprooted a plantation of Dutch iris and imparted crooked lines to the perennial beds from which they have never fully recovered. I worked in New York in those days, and when I came up for weekends my first wish was naturally to see the garden —a wish strongly opposed by the family, who offered me drinks, produced piles of mail, announced that we had to leave immediately for a dinner twenty miles away, anything to keep me from a tour of inspection. It was, they explained, Mr. R.'s canny habit to get his job done between five and six A.M., long before anyone was around to stop him. By breakfast time, the little heaps of plants he had pulled up were already past saving, the cement already setting between the bricks laid in the wrong place. Nothing one could say or do made any impression. I fired him in a blazing passion, but when we meet, which is often, he beams upon me and invariably passes a pleasant remark about the weather.

He was followed by A., who was, as they say, right off the boat. He spoke only Portuguese. I addressed him in Spanish, which he seemed to understand. Or I thought he did until I found him mowing the grass strip in front of the house, the grass-catcher not on the mower, which was blasting a steady stream of damp cuttings onto the façade. When this was pointed out, he smiled dreamily and moved into the street, the mower still going. I watched him cover a half-block of naked asphalt before I led him gently to the back door and paid him off.

He, as I remember it, was followed by Mr. H., of impeccable Yankee lineage—no language trouble there, and he was handy too, could make or mend anything; and the most remarkable painter I ever knew: Any object painted by him, including the house, stayed pristine for a decade. But Mr. H. had two problems. He weighed close to four hundred pounds, and he was mad, certifiably so, poor man, for he had done time. It showed in his stream-of-consciousness talk—which flowed on and on without pause or relevance and was distracting until one learned to tune out—and in a tendency to paranoid outbursts, which one also learned to ignore. His weight caused him to adopt some peculiar methods as well. He weeded, for example, in the reclining position of those stout riverine gods on Roman fountains, and dug in the same attitude, using a small trowel. I remember him attacking in this manner three large, well-rooted shrubs I wanted removed. It took a week. Mr. H. stayed with me for five or six years, getting fatter and crazier every year, until he retired at his own request, fuming over some fancied slight.

It occurs to me that I attract the mentally unbalanced. Or perhaps their therapists have advised them to take up outdoor work? There was the beautiful young Italian, a veritable Donatello with black curly hair and a bronze torso we saw a lot of because he liked to bare it while he worked. He arrived in a Cadillac of immense size, did little work but talked a lot about trips he intended to make, businesses he meant to start, and often asked to use the telephone. He was eventually arrested for having tried to murder his mistress, and though he was given a suspended sentence it seemed better not to have him around.

Yet another case, that of B. B., was an authentic tragedy. This nice man, who seemed perfectly normal, was the father of children and what is quite rare, made a point of saying how much he liked gardening. He killed himself a few weeks after he had agreed to see me through a summer. It was such a shock I wracked my brains trying to remember some missing clue to his state of mind. We had put in some roses and fruit trees together, and in these shared chores one learns, or senses, quite a lot about the other person—something of his sympathies and his attitude toward life—and yet no inkling of his despair had reached me. If anything I had the impression he was enjoying himself.

I was guilty of a common fallacy: We all, I think, tend to imagine that the people who work for us take the same satisfaction we do in a happy effect achieved, a heavy chore got through. Rarely is it so. Why should B. B. have looked forward to taking care of *my* garden, planting *my* fruit trees? To him, it was just a part-time job, a way to earn some extra cash for a few months. Had he been a professional, it might have been different. In that case his careerist's pride would have been involved. But B. B. was a machinist, not a nurseryman or an arborist; and that has been true of all my helpers. They all belong to the ranks of the temporarily unemployed or they are moonlighting. Not one of them has ever had the slightest knowledge of horticulture, or ever acquired it—not even my dear A. V., with me for five years, who truly did love the garden, loved, that is, dressing it up to look its best, especially when company was expected, and did mysteriously acquire a passion for building compost heaps, but never learned to identify a single flower, bush or tree or any of the techniques connected with growing them. And, as he often told me, the men at "the shop" thought he was nuts to get such a kick out of working here.

Gardening is so little esteemed in this country that I can't imagine where or how someone who wanted to study it as a profession would go for instruction. It's a vicious circle. Those who, like me, need help can't find it and so are forced to cut down on their plantings, abandon the flowers or the vegetables or both, thus diminishing the potential job market for those who might choose to earn a living at it. There is a gap here, and some of the young have undertaken to fill it—at exorbitant rates. They are innocent of the most elementary techniques, barely know a rose from a cabbage, or even how to mow a lawn properly. Their tools are a rotary mower, an electric hedge cutter and a pickup truck. At best, they are the maturing flower children of the 1960's, still wearing their beards and pigtails; at worst, grasping little entrepreneurs who know just enough to demand $18 an hour. So for me it has to be the lunatic fringe, and now and again I am lucky—as with A. V., whose only noticeable eccentricity was a tendency to fall off ladders and out of trees. Right now, I am in a hopeful phase. My current helper is a young man sound in wind, limb, and as far as I know, mind, and a whiz at getting through the work. But he is also a talented sculptor, and his pieces are beginning to sell so well that I foresee the day when he will think twice about raking up twenty bushels of apples.

—from *Green Thoughts*, 1981

Gardeners

BY KATHERINE MANSFIELD

Out in the garden,
Out in the windy, swinging dark,
Under the trees and over the flower-beds,
Over the grass and under the hedge border,
Someone is sweeping, sweeping,
Some old gardener.
Out in the windy, swinging dark,
Someone is secretly putting in order,
Someone is creeping, creeping.

—from *Out in the Garden,* 1922

On the Defiance
of Gardeners

BY HENRY MITCHELL

As I write this, on June 29, it's about time for another summer
storm to smash the garden to pieces, though it may hold off until
the phlox, tomatoes, daylilies, and zinnias are in full sway.

I detect an unwholesome strain in gardeners here, who
keep forgetting how very favorable our climate is, and who seem
almost on the verge of ingratitude. Disaster, they must learn, is the
normal state of any garden, but every time there is wholesale ruin
we start sounding off—gardeners here—as if it were terribly un-
just. Go to any of those paradise-type gardens elsewhere, however, and see what they put up with in the way of weather, and you
will stop whimpering. What is needed around here is more grit in
gardeners.

Now I guess there is no garden in the world more dream-
worthy than the one at Tresco Abbey in the Scilly Isles. It rarely
approaches freezing there, off the mild coast of England, and won-

ders abound. Palms grow luxuriantly against soft old stonework, medieval in origin, and there is hardly an exotic rarity of New Zealand or South Africa or Madeira that does not flourish. And yet they can have their daffodils, too, for it never gets hot in those islands, either; and if you view such a garden in the long slanting light of a summer's late afternoon, you will think you have got to heaven in spite of yourself. Indeed, almost any garden, if you see it at just the right moment, can be confused with paradise. But even the greatest gardens, if you live with them day after decade, will throw you into despair. At Tresco, that sheltered wonderland, they wake up some mornings to discover 500 trees are down— the very shelter belts much damaged. The cost of cleanup is too grim to dwell on, but even worse is the loss of not mere lousy Norway maples, but of rare cherished specimens that were a wonder to see in flower.

Or there may be—take the great gardens of Gloucestershire—a drought, and the law forbids you to run the hose. Not just a little dry spell, either, but one going on month after month. There you sit in your garden, watching even the native oaks dry up, and as for the rarities imported at such cost, and with such dreams, from the moist Himalayas, the less said of their silent screams the better.

Or take another sort of garden, in which the land to begin with is a collection of rusting bedsprings and immortal boots. Old shoes simply do not rot, in my opinion, but just stay there forever. The chief growth the gardener finds (I am speaking now of the great garden of Sissinghurst in Kent) is brambles and bracken and dock, maybe broken up by patches of stinging nettles. Amenities include the remains of an old pig sty. You convert it, let's say, into one of the sweetest gardens of the world, with roundels of clipped yew and a little alley of lindens, rising over a wide walk, almost a terrace, of concrete cast in big blocks (not one in a thousand knew it was concrete) with spaces for a riot of primroses and spring bulbs, bursting out everywhere in lemon and scarlet and gentian and ivory. The lindens all die. The pavement has to be replaced. The primroses start dying out—they develop a sickness, they wear out the soil, and no mulches of manure, no coddling of any sort will preserve them. So you grub out the dying and start anew with something else.

Wherever humans garden magnificently, there are magnificent heartbreaks. It may be 40 heifers break through the hedge after a spring shower and (undiscovered for many hours) trample the labor of many years into uniform mire. It may be the gardener has nursed along his camellias for 25 years, and in one night of February they are dead. How can that be? Well, it can be. You have one of the greatest gardens of the Riviera, and one night the dam of the reservoir breaks. The floor of the house is covered with a foot of mud once the water subsides. The reservoir was built at endless labor and cost, since the garden would die without water from it. And now it is gone, and in the flood everything has gone with it. Be sure that is not the day to visit that great garden.

I never see a great garden (even in my mind's eye, which is the best place to see great gardens around here) but I think of the calamities that have visited it, unsuspected by the delighted visitor who supposes it must be nice to garden here.

It is not nice to garden anywhere. Everywhere there are violent winds, startling once-per-five-centuries floods, unprecedented droughts, record-setting freezes, abusive and blasting heats never known before. There is no place, no garden, where these terrible things do not drive gardeners mad.

I smile when I hear the ignorant speak of lawns that take 300 years to get the velvet look (for so the ignorant think). It is far otherwise. A garden is very old (though not yet mature) at 40 years, and already, by that time, many things have had to be replaced, many treasures have died, many great schemes abandoned, many temporary triumphs have come to nothing and worse than nothing. If I see a garden that is very beautiful, I know it is a new garden. It many have an occasional surviving wonder—a triumphant old cedar—from the past, but I know the intensive care is of the present.

So there is no point dreading the next summer storm that, as I predict, will flatten everything. Nor is there any point dreading the winter, so soon to come, in which the temperature will drop to ten below zero and the ground freezes forty inches deep and we all say there never was such a winter since the beginning of the world. There have been such winters; there will be more.

Now the gardener is the one who has seen everything ruined so many times that (even as his pain increases with each loss) he comprehends—truly knows—that where there was a garden once, it can be again, or where there never was, there yet can be a garden so that all who see it say, "Well, you have favorable conditions here. Everything grows for you." Everything grows for everybody. Everything dies for everybody, too.

There are no green thumbs or black thumbs. There are only gardeners and non-gardeners. Gardeners are the ones who ruin after ruin get on with the high defiance of nature herself, creating, in the very face of her chaos and tornado, the bower of roses and the pride of irises. It sounds very well to garden a "natural way." You may see the natural way in any desert, any swamp, any leech-filled laurel hell. Defiance, on the other hand, is what makes gardeners.

—from *The Essential Earthman*, 1981

Days Are Different

BY GEOFFREY B. CHARLESWORTH

An Ideal Day

I get up at six. It must be late May or early June because the sun is just about to rise above the hills on the east side of the house. It rained during the night; there is no need to worry about watering the seedpots. Nobody is visiting; there is no need to shave. I'm downstairs exactly in time for the weather forecast, avoiding the Dow Jones average, baseball scores, rock music, and ads—it will be dry and sunny with a high of 70°. I drink my orange juice while waiting for the kettle to boil, then slice a perfectly ripe banana on cereal. In the greenhouse, after breakfast, last night's transplants are sitting in water soaking. I put these pots into trays and carry them outside to sit on a table until I am ready to move them to a coldframe. The air is cool after the rain and the grass wet so there is no urgency to cross the lawn and look at plants; in any case 6:30 is a favorite mosquito time.

This makes potting in the greenhouse very attractive. I

remembered last night to bring into the greenhouse several pots of seedlings ready to transplant. All of them have between ten and twenty well-spaced seedlings, each with two good leaves and some with more. All of them are very desirable, being new to cultivation, new to me, or things I want to either try again myself or give away to friends. All of them have pretty leaves and strong stems. There is enough compost ready mixed from last night to get me through the first three or four species, but I have to mix up another batch to finish off all the pots of seedlings waiting to be done. Wood pigeons are cooing, robins are making assertive noises, a white-throated sparrow sings my favorite song. The potting goes well, the roots separate easily and I end up with four kitty litter trays of transplants soaking in an inch of water. By now it is 8:30 and I retire to the kitchen to drink hot chocolate, write labels, and record the transplant activity in my seedlist.

At 9:00 I have finished putting the labels in the pots, the sun has warmed up the air and the grass while still damp is no longer soaking wet. It is gardening time. There is a tray of plants ready to be planted out, they are all big enough and require the same growing conditions, so I carry them to a suitable bed that needs refurbishing. I return for tools: buckets, claw, trowel, spade, scissors, kneeling pad, fertilizer. I weed the area, plant the whole batch, go to the pump for water, water them in, go back to the parking lot for buckwheat hulls (or gravel or whatever mulch seems right) and mulch the planted area. It is now 10:15; a good time to take photographs. The camera is loaded and I get some brilliant shots of a new plant flowering for the first time. I check the label for the name. The label is there behind the plant and unbroken. The name is visible. I write the name in a little notebook where I shall find it when the slides come back. I take other pictures and find I can remember the names of the plants or find a legible label. On the way around the garden I take note of all the plants in bud, admire the ones reaching full beauty, say goodbye to the ones going over and take note of the ones going to seed. It's 10:45 and time to open a can for lunch. Norman gets the mail. Over lunch we read the mail, which consists of letters from other gardeners containing fresh seed of short-lived viability, a few checks, and a notice that my pension will be increased next month.

After lunch is the best time to look at seedpots for germination—excitement without exertion. Since it is late in the season I can't really expect too much but end up with over twenty, including some pulsatillas (these seem to germinate erratically) and iris (which usually germinate late) and an unexpected kniphofia. I arrange the pots alphabetically and enter the germinations in my seed record. It is now noon and the weather delightful so I decide to edge a bed. Once wielding a spade I am overcome by an impulse to make the bed larger. I start cutting sod and laying it upside down where the extension is to be. This is so absorbing I swiftly lose all sense of guilt about doing something I shall be later asked to explain and justify. By 2:00 I can see the new bed taking shape and I feel I can leave it and take time out for tea. At 2:30 tea is over, the sun is strong and a spell in the wood is indicated. I find a shady bed to weed and it seems a good opportunity to finally learn the names of a few ferns. Instead I barely glance at the labels, admire the varied patterns of the ferns as I weed around them, mulch them to make them look pretty, and face up to the reality that I shall never remember any name with four parts for more than a minute. After the ferns I visit the bog and note that *Cypripedium reginae* has six shoots coming up, the dodecatheons look marvelous even though they are going over, the *Lobelia* x *vedrariensis* is still alive, and the mimulus is coming back. I start the return trip back to the house, weeding the ornamental grasses on the way. I am back in the kitchen by 4:30 and think about dinner. Fortunately there are leftovers, so it means microwave and not real cooking. By 5:30 the eating process is finished for the day and I relax watching the weather on TV. At 6:00 it is time to go out again. The mosquitoes are still quiet and I can get in an hour's mowing.

At 7:00 I am back in the greenhouse and go on transplanting until sunset. After sunset I write labels. Finally at 8:30 I have a shower and read or write until 10:30, with maybe a half hour of TV trash sandwiched in there. An ideal day would be followed by a night of sound uninterrupted sleep. But there are very few days like this; most of the time I have . . .

A Less than Ideal Day

It is 6:00, already hot, and a bit sticky. It hasn't rained for days. A New York friend called last night threatening to visit so I have to shave so as not to appear uncouth. Breakfast is spoiled— the orange juice ran out. This means going in to town—what a waste of time. I go into the greenhouse, the screen door was left open, and I hear the buzz of a wasp and the low scream of a mosquito. I forgot to bring in any pots of seedlings so I have to go out to the frames to find something ready to transplant. The pots feel clammy and as I search for half a dozen pots I get bitten. The Jiffy mix bins are empty. I go to the barn and carry back a fortypound bag to the greenhouse. Sand too is low so I bring in four buckets from the sandpile. By now it is 8:00 and I feel I haven't even started.

There seems to be something wrong with each of the pots I brought in. One of them is crowded with seedlings too closely sown, but when I knock it out the roots are obviously not long enough. The compost it was sown in was too sandy and the mass starts to fall apart. I rescue a few clumps but the tiny single seedlings are not worth potting. The first drop of rain would annihilate them. The next pot has three large seedlings and several small ones. Shall I do it and risk losing all the little ones? I ponder the alternatives and decide to wait until they are a little bigger. The next pot is *Alyssum saxatile*. Why on earth did I sow these seeds? My own garden has a rich variety of yellows and I don't really need any more plants of this useful but commonplace species. I remember the plant sale and what a good plant this is for beginners so, a little grudgingly, I spend time potting six of them. I try a campanula next but the leaves have become entangled and extreme care is needed not to break them off. The roots too have grown together and are hard to pull apart so I take an unconscionable length of time to get just a few plants potted. By now it is 8:30 and time for hot chocolate. Today it tastes sickeningly sweet and I resolve never to drink the stuff again.

The forecast promised thirty percent chance of rain tomorrow so we use this as an excuse to postpone marketing. So no orange juice tomorrow either. At 9:00 I am ready to go outside. I decide against changing into rubbers. The grass is still wet with a heavy dew and my sneakers and socks are soon soaking. I carry a tray of plants to a bed ready for a planting-out session. The black fly are back and I feel something bite my ankle while another gets me behind the left ear. I put down the tray, swipe my ear, and bend down to tuck my pants inside my socks. Too late — and the bottoms of the pants are wet through. I deliver the tray and go back to the barn for planting tools: a claw and a trowel. I go back to the bed and realize I shall need a kneeling mat so back to the greenhouse. Now I see that the open space I had my eye on has a label — *Roscoea!* Is it still alive? Shall I risk digging it up? I remember roscoea comes up late and decide to try another bed. I find room for one plant. But now insects have gathered into a small cloud around my head and I have to retreat in haste and discomfort, leaving the tools on the ground. I go back to the barn and pick up a spade to do some edging. The bed I choose is on stony ground and the spade soon hits a big one. The next half hour is spent getting it out. Wet grass, turned soil, and human sweat attract the maddening hum of deer fly. Usually you can let one land on your wrist and give it a biff with your other hand. With hands covered with mud this turns out to be unpleasant and ineffectual so I leave the rest of the edging for another day.

It is lunchtime and we are reduced to peanut butter. The mail is junk and bills. There is no newspaper. I remember a plant I have to photograph—*Eritrichium howardii*—and grab the camera and go out looking for the raised bed I think it is in. Eventually I find it placed about a foot away from the edge. The raised bed has a border fully planted and there is nowhere to kneel without doing serious damage to at least one plant. If I stand I am too far away, if I sprawl with my wrists on the bed I have no control. I settle for kneeling.

There are an infinite number of ways a day can be imperfect and this day has been discouraging. It could have been an accident with a clumsy hose, a broken spade, an elaborate attempt to collect seed that turned out to be unripe. The worst category of mishap is the kind that forces an action you really don't want to do. The mowing machine breaks down, an animal digs a large hole in a bed or digs up a plant and leaves it on the surface with exposed roots, you run out of sand, Jiffy mix, pots, labels, or something else vital, you notice a plant wilting in the coldframe and have to stop whatever you are doing to water, a bird gets caught in the chipmunk trap, UPS arrives with twenty bags you have to help unload, a kind neighbor brings bales of hay and dumps them in the wrong place, visitors arrive just as you are transplanting a pot of tricky *Eriogonum* seedlings, a storm breaks a few branches that crash down on one of the beds. These are major events that seem sent by Jehovah to test the patience of the Jobs of gardening. But most of what makes a day less than perfect is lack of planning, forgetfulness, willfulness. In other words it is your fault. But there is also . . .

A Third Kind of Day

You may have to spend the day in bed ill, you may have to go to a mall to buy clothes, you may have to take a visiting relative to an art gallery, or you may have to go to the dentist for a root canal job, or attend a birthday party, you might win a lottery, you may have to leave for a vacation. These are the experiences of a third kind that novelists and movie script writers celebrate, along with sex and crime, as the fabric of life. I suppose they are right in a way. Gardening is nothing compared to a major operation or a declaration of war. But essentially the novelists are wrong. The dramas of life certainly affect its course, but unless your life is in fact a soap opera of sex and crime these catastrophic events are few and far between. How often do you go to a mall? Uneventful living takes up most of our time. Gardening is part of it, possibly a trivial part to the rest of the world, but by no means less important to the gardener than the big events.

A perfect day for anybody is most likely one of the in-between days when nothing happens. For nongardeners it may mean a smooth commute to work with a great Danish pastry at coffee break and the boss in a good mood. For gardeners it may be not misplacing your secateurs. On a day when something *important* happens and no gardening is possible I turn off. As I drive down Norfolk Road I stop thinking of seedlings, botanical Latin, mulches, and mowing. The resentment at having to leave paradise has already been lived through as part of the anticipation and has tempered the pleasure (or annoyance) that doing something important might have promised. As I lie in bed with flu, surrounded by boxes of Kleenex, or sleep off the pain of an operation, the garden hardly exists. Not even making garden design doodles has any magic. By the time gardening intrudes itself on my consciousness again I know I am nearly well.

A garden can be very accommodating in this way, especially if you have to leave it for an extended period of time. The garden exists even though you ignore it and when you finally get back to it you have to not only catch up with the obvious cleanup chores, you have to rethink your whole plan. Is this patch of weeds a place you cleared in order to plant or has everything died? It takes a full day of this disorientation to grasp the situation and recollect what the garden is all about. When you do you are horrified at the gross changes a few days away from the garden can bring about, and then pleased that even weedy, you love it and are glad to be back. Even if you are only away for a day some alienation takes place and it isn't until you have picked up a spade and made a few false starts that it all comes back to you and you take possession of your domain once again. On an ideal day you don't lose touch; you belong to the process and everything you do seems right.

—from *A Gardener Obsessed*, 1994

What Is a Garden, Anyway?

BY ABBY ADAMS

There are as many kinds of gardens as there are gardeners, and they define themselves across sharp aesthetic and philosophical lines: utility versus beauty; vegetables versus ornamentals; chemicals versus organics; formal style versus naturalistic. Different countries breed different gardeners.

In America, when people ask "Do you have a garden?" they usually aren't thinking of perennials, or roses, or azaleas, and they certainly aren't thinking of expanses of raked sand; they're thinking of tomatoes and lettuces, neatly lined up in rows.

In England they're more likely to mean flowers and ornamentals. Gardening in England is a hobby, about midway on the social scale between throwing darts and composing sonnets. Even the growing of vegetables has been turned into a sport, a quest for record-breaking fruit—twenty-pound tomatoes, half-ton marrows, three-foot-long carrots.

"Gardening is a luxury occupation," writes Vita Sackville-West; and the practitioner "one of the few people left in this distressful world to carry on the tradition of elegance and charm." In our heart of hearts, we American gardeners may think of ourselves as artists, but we'd rather eat out of the compost heap than admit it. We're much more comfortable growing organic melons, or striking a blow for ethnobotanical diversity, than we are with Beauty.

We are also uneasy with the notion that as gardeners we are working *against* nature.

Gardeners are—let's face it—control freaks. Who else would willingly spend his leisure hours wresting weeds out of the ground, blithely making life or death decisions about living beings, moving earth from here to there, changing the course of waterways? The more one thinks about it, the odder it seems; this compulsion to remake a little corner of the planet according to some plan or vision.

Some people are made very uncomfortable by the realization that as gardeners we are playing God. These are the people who plant butterfly gardens and grow wildflowers and find beauty and even nutrition in their weeds. These are the people who rip up their lawns to grow native trees. But the very act of planting and growing and ripping up puts us at odds with nature. A garden is not nature. Isn't it better to acknowledge this and accept the responsibility than to try and duck it by pretending that one is Mother Nature's handmaiden (or handyman)? There's not really that much difference between an ecologically correct meadow and the manicured, not-a-petal-out-of-place flower beds that surround the war memorial in the village green.

A garden, then, is a finite place, in which a gardener (or

several gardeners) has created, working with or against nature, a plot whose intention it is to provide pleasure; possibly in the form of beauty, possibly in the form of cabbages—and possibly, beautiful cabbages.

And nature? Nature is what wins in the end.

—from *The Gardener's Gripe Book*, 1995

Sunday in the Garden
with Weeds

BY SARA STEIN

The National Audubon Society, speaking through the *New York Times* on the popularity of birdwatching, offered an interesting aside on gardening: it has become, the society claims, "the nation's second-most-popular passive sport."

I don't know what to make of it. Gardening gives me blisters. Also tired muscles. And aching joints. I can agree that birders stay still to watch birds, and I call that passive, but I admit to sitting still for a beer only after there's a heap of weeds to say I deserve it. "Sport" is an unusual description of gardening, but not without merit. Webster's III says sport is "something that is a source of pleasant diversion," and I'll buy that if Audubon will buy my calluses.

Or perhaps they knew my mother. My mother gardened in a costume. She wore a suit of nubby white linen, white kid shoes, and a navy-blue bandanna. She carried a basket and a set of miniature tools. She weeded pots of petunias. I would have thought her gentility out of fashion these many years if I hadn't noticed for sale, year after year, the same cute sets of tools the size of party favors.

I have found the sport of gardening lusty, sweaty, and hard. Sometimes I try to get around its central issue by doing what gardeners do in picture books. I bring home from the nursery little pots of flowers. Then I pose for my own future recollection as a pansy planter. Unhappily, a single hour is enough to plant three dozen pots of plants. What next? Maybe I treat myself to some pruning, which can, under the best of circumstances, be performed like an artist at his canvas, with many steppings back to cock the head, then circle round and again step forth to snip a twig or so. Or I might cut a bunch of roses, bring them into the house, arrange them in a bowl, pour a beer. But I know that's cheating.

The real work is weeding.

On mornings of determination I load the cart with an arsenal of gardening tools: loppers and pruners, rake, spade, fork, and hand tools, as well as hoes. This is because weeding is like housecleaning. Cleaning reveals messes one hadn't known were there. The alternative to setting out with many tools is to set out with one, and one by one fetch all the others anyway.

It is a Sunday in spring. I start in the herb garden because it's about as easy as petunia pots, and the closest thing to genteel around here. The herb garden is basically brick, with rows of square planting areas that hold one plant each of large herbs such as rosemary or tarragon, or as many as half a dozen skinny plants like basil. The twelve squares, plus several narrow beds along the sides, quickly fill with whatever is planted in them. They can be weeded in ladylike fashion because there are no weeds to speak of.

So I begin picture-book style, with a hand fork. The hand fork is to loosen the dirt around the herbs so that the few small weeds that may have come up can be plucked out by hand. But already there are complications. A dandelion has snookered its taproot under the brick edging where the fork won't pry it loose. This calls for a dandelion tool, a long-shafted hand weeder with a cutting end V-shaped like the quill of an arrow. It is designed for severing taprooted weeds several inches below ground level, too deep for them to resprout from the remaining root. The implement is an old joke among dandelions. The joke goes like this: "What is a dandelion tool for?" "For reproducing dandelions." In fact, I have not found a depth at which their taproot fails to resprout, but I continue to hope.

The suckers that have grown up from the roots of the lilac tree at the corner of the house are no better than weeds. I snip them off with loppers. Over the winter a purple sage bit the dust; I dig it out with a spade. Then I notice mint escaping into the cracks between bricks. That problem is worth a mental note to check the supply of herbicide. No tool can pry mint from a crack.

The herb garden is enclosed. Three sides are formed by the white stucco walls of the house and garage, the fourth, at the south end, by a low stone wall. Originally it and another walled garden on the opposite side of the house were to be the only cultivated areas on the property. The idea was sane. The natural meadow with its rolling contours and rock outcroppings was lovely. We could garden in what amounted to the backyard of a brownstone; the rest would be background.

Then we thought to clean up the background a bit, comb its hair, straighten its clothes. Farmers working the land had built stone walls of the larger rocks they had dug out of the fields; smaller ones had been tossed out of the way onto the rock outcroppings. We started there. Baring them back to their original glacier-scrubbed sculpture bared whatever soil had since accumulated in depressions and fissures. Weeds moved in. We replaced them with shrubs—junipers and ilex in a small outcropping, and, in a larger one, junipers combined with blueberries and Siberian iris.

The only troublesome weed in these older gardens is lawn. Lawn is, in fact, a weed along the edges of almost any garden. A lawn is a weed because the same grass rhizomes that spread to form a dense turf within a lawn also spread beyond the lawn wherever they can. Authorities claim grass root incursions can be stopped by sinking plastic edging strips sold for that purpose, by digging a narrow trench and filling it with gravel, by mulching the garden bed heavily, or by barricading it with brick, stone, or railroad ties.

I haven't found any such solution workable. Plastic stripping is awful stuff to get into the ground. The trench has to be as straight and as level as you want the edge to be, and even if you've gotten the stripping just right it heaves with frost the following winter and emerges looking like a serpent. Maybe strips work in the South. As for a gravel barrier, grass rhizomes penetrate it as mint penetrates the gravel between the bricks, or as grass grows in a driveway. Bricks don't work either, nor do stones; both have spaces between them. I haven't tried railroad ties. Why wouldn't grass sneak underneath what amounts to no more than a square log? Certainly grass sneaks through mulch.

I edge instead. I love to edge. There's a rhythm to it— *stamp*, one two, *lift*, one two, *slide*, one two, *stamp*. Each stamp on the edging tool makes a crunch as the blade cuts through trespassing turf. One steps right along, never lifting the working foot from its place on the edger, not moving too fast, just edging along. The tool, the edger, is a half-moon-shaped, flat blade on a short handle. One steps on it like a spade to plunge the blade into the turf, cutting through it to the soil below. The angle, however, is different than for digging. A spade is usually held at a slant; the edger is held straight up.

The curved border of the smaller rock garden measures

about forty feet, and takes ten minutes to edge. Before I got accustomed to the tool, I used it like a spade to pry out each chunk of turf before continuing the line. Now I never pry and barely lift the blade, but ride it like a one-footed pogo stick until the line is finished. The severed clods are easy to pick up and bang out after the cutting's done. If grass has so obscured the line that I'm not sure where it is, I lay out a hose to the contour I want and work along it. In straight borders I lay out the line with stakes and string.

Edging is a three-time thing: once in spring and two more times over the summer season. To me spring edging is an opening ceremony, a ritual commitment to make the interior of a garden as clean as its edge is crisp. It is also a way of avoiding getting dirt under the fingernails right off the bat.

Now the work goes underground in the sinuous box and ilex border that runs along a stone retaining wall to one side of the outcropping. The border is only a summer old; the shrubs are silly bumps in a bed that is mostly mulch; ugly weeds have arisen from unseen seeds and scraps of root. Quackgrass has snaked between rocks in the retaining wall, following soil-filled crevices like blind vines. Sorrel has networked beneath the mulch. Bindweed has begun. I spot young nutsedge, infant garlic. I don't know why gardeners are told to hoe weeds like these. There is no sense in cutting quackgrass stems to bits, when every bit will sprout anew. Sorrel's russet roots web through mulch and under it, sending new plants upward every inch or so. Hacking it out means mixing mulch with soil, bringing more hidden seeds to the surface, and still not getting to the bottom of the weeds. There's not a chance that the creeping roots of bindweed can be eradicated by cultivation, for they break to sprouting bits. A nutsedge's roots are just as fragile, but they are threadlike and end in a nut-brown tuber, or in a new nutsedge that has just grown from it. Tiny garlic bulbs are merely spread by hoeing.

Such weeds must be loosened from the soil first with a digging fork, then tracked down by hand through the soil as Theseus followed a thread to negotiate the Labyrinth.

A digging fork is a stout, short-handled tool with four flat tines about a foot long. It can be used for turning soil over, as in a vegetable garden in the spring, but for weeding I use it delicately to nudge the soil loose from roots without breaking them, and without disturbing the mulch on top. I start at the edge of a patch of quackgrass, push the fork in straight and deep, tilt the handle gently until the earth gives a bit, then withdraw the tines. I do this all through the patch, and for some distance beyond.

Then I crouch down and begin to tickle my fingers from the crown of the grass plant down into the earth along a tough white rhizome, probing with my fingers, feeling out its wiry path, tugging carefully with my other hand at the coarse grass blades at the surface, pulling the snaky thing bit by bit out of the soil all along its shallow run. Often a single rhizome extends for a yard or more. New quackgrass plants sprout at regular intervals, pale shoots still buried, others growing green and strong in the sun. The rhizome ends in a point so sharp one can almost pierce the flesh with it; if the end is blunt, it has been broken and some portion still remains behind regenerating itself. This is only one rhizome of perhaps half a dozen, all awling the soil in different directions, radiating out from the parent like the stems of a sunken spider plant. The patch may prove to be a single plant, and even widespread patches may be connected. I feel an urge to keep such dug-up monsters, trophies of a successful hunt.

I don't wear gloves when hunting roots. A gloved rooter is as absurd as a blindfolded birder. It is the hands that learn to identify weed roots, and, through years of intimacy, predict their course, forestall their progress. I suppose I look foolish backside up and hands burrowing. But I am not seeing that. I am visualizing through unseeing hands a subterranean forest webbed in root, and sinuous with creeping stems. I track my prey through the fibrous underpinnings of a box bush, among the tubers of a daylily, and feel the difference. My fingers are wanderers underground, explorers in a landscape where I have never been.

I hit a snag. A spreading grass has grown through the crown of a daylily from which it is not to be tugged. Regretfully I turn its subterranean world upside down and expose it. Lifted and shaken free of soil, the bright white grass roots show up against the buff bunch of daylily roots and, not expecting attack from this direction, slip easily down and out, blades and all. Of course, one must then replant the plant.

Sorrel roots are strange. They are webby, rubbery, often rusty in color. They feel like fungi. The weed spreads particularly through mulch, sometimes so shallowly that parted fingers pushed along the soil below accumulated garlands of sorrel plants, like a rake dragged through seaweed. If the roots go no deeper than the mulch, it isn't even necessary to fork them loose. But if they go deeper, or if there is no mulch layer, I must first shake up the network of connected plants, jiggle them loose by inserting the fork beneath them parallel to the ground surface and jounce it up and down until soil falls away from the sorrel plants. Then the whole network can be combed up with the fingers.

The "nuts" for which nutsedge is named are tubers that break from the fragile underground stems as easily as a spent petal drops from a blossom. Each tuber sprouts a new nutsedge, connected with the original plant if the tuber has not been detached, independent if it has. I loosen nutsedge with a forking technique halfway between that used for quackgrass and that for sorrel. I shove in the fork at a medium angle six inches or so from what I take to be the center of spread, then tilt it back lightly to lift the clod of soil on it, then repeat the motion throughout the infested area. The idea is so to free the nutsedge's entire root mass that the plants can be lifted without their snow-white, tendril-tender rhizomes' being broken. I cup both hands, fingers spread, and plunge them into the ground on either side of a loosened plant. Then I lift, wiggling fingers and shaking hands like an animated sieve. A tearing sound accompanying this operation is pieces breaking away to generate new nutsedges.

Bindweed always breaks to pieces underground. It has about the consistency of beansprouts. The pale fragments actually resemble beansprouts when they resprout, as they all do. What's more, not even a mole could follow a bindweed root to its end, twenty feet or so beneath the garden bed. Before a bindweed has gotten that far, it can be dissected from the soil by removing mulch, excavating carefully with a hand fork and trowel, watching with an eagle eye, and snatching fast at any glint of white.

One must also use the eyes to extract wild garlic. Tempting as it is to simply pull them up like scallions, the tiny bulbs that form around the larger central one remain huddled in the soil. I use a very narrow trowel, the kind designed for bedding seedlings or burying small bulbs. I stick it in close to the plant, aim it straight down, and push it deep to dig the weed out with a plug of soil surrounding it. Then I put the plug in my palm and tease it apart to free the nest of bulbs. The fussiness is worth it. With wild garlic, as with all cloning weeds, if you have gotten out all of it, it is unlikely to return. That's why the old outcroppings, as opposed to the new borders, need so little work. I have conquered the clones.

My husband never does the weeding. Weeding is finicky work. It requires an overestimation of the importance of detail, a near-sighted view of things. Marty is an architect; he sees the big view: masses, contours, heights, spaces. I have an eye for weeds. I can discern a lambsquarter in the lamb's ear, a sedge among the daylilies. But it makes me mad, this God-given division of labor. I pluck and grub in a rage as Marty the Master Builder adds a fine flat rock to the growing curve of the long wall he is rebuilding to retain the terrace that will be the birch grove underplanted with azaleas that I will weed, and that will be woven with grass paths that I will edge. My fury drives my foot against the fork, forces my fingers to their grave, and all the while I am getting madder still, realizing that anger makes my weeding all the more vigorous, thorough, niggling, and exemplary. The good girl, the good wife, the perfect weeder.

Gradually, speeches screeching in my brain are interrupted by images. I glimpse my mother, who used to practice such speeches aloud while soaking in the bathtub, and whose basket of petunia weeds was always left coyly on the doorstep for my father to dispose of when he took out the garbage. I instead am soaking in my own sweat, leaving heaps of weeds destroying vital contours, leaving them for Marty to pick up. At least I am within tradition. I begin to consider which I would rather be doing, hauling rocks or pulling weeds. The garden is looking good. I rake a sodden heap of leaves from under a box bush, shear back winter-damaged ilex tips, saw off an asymmetric limb from one of a pair of cherry trees that arch over the steps descending through the middle of the border down toward the pond. Marty built those steps. Weeding is good for the soul.

—from *My Weeds: A Gardener's Botany,* 1988

In Search of Plants

BY THOMAS C. COOPER

With the possible exception of squirrels, gardeners may be the most acquisitive creatures on earth. Even well-balanced gardeners order a good number of seeds each year "just to try," and few can leave a nursery without buying at least three items they did not need. Led on by catalogs, books, and the stories of friends, they will pursue a good plant for years.

Some gardeners lose their hearts to one plant. If it is hostas they fancy, they will grow all the kinds that garden and checkbook allow and will not sleep soundly if a shipment of new hybrids is due from Japan. Other gardeners focus their attention on plants from a particular country and are not content until they have grown or at least seen everything from, say, China. They will save up vacation time and money, then desert family and friends to spend three weeks overseas gathering choice plants, in the mean-time collecting rare forms of dysentery and tapeworm as well.

I recently made a brief trip around England with two friends who like plants of all colors and denominations. Their appetite is insatiable, and they have worked their collection into a wonderful garden in Vermont. When we decided last winter to make the trip, my friends calmly announced that they intended to bring plants home. This is something I have never attempted myself, for I lacked the nerve or patience to tackle the labyrinthian bureaucracy that deals out permits, to say nothing of the likelihood of the plants dying slow and gruesome deaths in a customs warehouse somewhere. None of this deterred my companions, who arrived in England with a bulging packet of permits. By the end of the first day the trunk of our rental car was half full of plants, and before long both the trunk and the rear seat resembled small gardens. I especially liked the placement of a large-leaved rhubarb next to a lightly variegated spirea.

Before we could send the plants home, we had to wash them and get them inspected. Like miners panning for gold, we carefully teased out every grain of soil from the root balls. Inspectors came and scrutinized the plants, which were naked but for a skimpy coating of peat moss. We then packed our certified-sanitary plants in two unassuming boxes and left them on a British Airways loading dock. We departed with a mixture of elation and sadness, the sort of feeling a parent has watching a child go off for the first day of school.

The plants reached their final destination one week later, after stopping in New York to overcome jet lag and the suspicions of more plant inspectors. All in all, the process required nearly fifty phone calls, four or five faxes, numerous letters, three boxes of plastic bags, and great quantities of time and money. But not only were the plants alive when they arrived, they looked like they had enough energy left to turn around and make the trip again. That seems a small price to pay for a few wonderful additions to the garden.

—from *Odd Lots*, 1995

How the Garden Grows and Grows

BY HENRY MITCHELL

A gardening friend of mine has quite lost her mind—not that it distresses her much—and no longer makes an effort to conceal her madness.

I estimate her garden to be twenty by twenty-two feet, and she started out all right a few years ago by paving the center with brick and acquiring a little table and four chairs, with a rose, a lilac, a camellia, a few lilies, a peony, a grape, and so on around the edges. Everyone thought she had done well. But of course it didn't last. At first she dissimulated about things, and was much given to saying, "Oh, I think you have seen the Japanese anemones, they've always been here." She said things of this sort when she had broken down and been tempted beyond her strength by a catalogue or garden center.

She was very bad about garden centers; we all noticed that from the beginning. She would go on some stated mission of acquiring a sack of peat moss, but would surreptitiously (entering stealthily at night, I suspect) bring home several flats of snapdragons and the Lord only knows what else. It got to the point where things were planted on top of each other, so of course many of them did not flourish greatly, and this gave her an excuse to yank them out.

"I cannot think why the platycodons did not perform this year," she would say, pretending to be puzzled about why they were no longer there and (suddenly) ten lily bulbs were.

But as time passed, she dropped all pretense. That much, at least, was a step in the right direction, no doubt.

It all came to a head when she converted a basement room (in which an unfortunate maid had once lived, it was said, though even in the old days there were laws against open cruelty, surely). This room has one small window, so she painted the whole thing white and installed enough special lights to illuminate the Capitol, and got someone to build a batch of stages on which she could set as many pots and flats of dirt as could be managed.

She no longer hid her packets of seed. They sat there in great rows. She had two hundred packets of seed at once — eggplant, tomatoes, thunbergias, snapdragons, zinnias, and endless other things.

"Do you think you have room for eggplants?" her saner friends would say — before it finally dawned on them that she knew she was mad, and did not wish to be sane.

"I've got some big pots for them," she would say in November. Sure enough, in February the eggplants would produce some tumescent objects which she said were eggplants, and which she proposed to eat, until somebody told her (for no good reason except that the eggplants looked loathsome) that if she ate them, they'd kill her, since they were obviously poisonous. She persisted and recently set great pots of eggplants on the brick pavement of the garden.

She whacked back the climbing roses to skeletons, sawed down the camellia and two young magnolias, ordered great quantities of asparagus, strawberries, and half-barrels, in which she said everything would fit beautifully. A fig, a plum, and a peach were supposed to live in barrels. As for the strawberries and blueberries, she said she was going to take up the bricks and build ziggurats where the table used to be, and on the little terraces, she said, the strawberries and much else would grow to beat the band.

She said it was silly to have all that space (about twelve feet square) just for people to lounge about drinking coffee and eating apricots. The only reason there are any bricks at all (the tiny paved area still remains) is that she could not figure how to take them up herself, and none of her friends would have any part in the project.

Once, in rather bitter jest, I suppose, someone offered her some little sequoia trees in pots. She accepted, but I never saw them planted out.

There is a vast space of wall, about twenty-eight inches wide, beyond the French windows, in which she planted a trumpet vine, a quite vigorous grape, and several clematis, and when they did not grow as rapidly as she thought they should, she filled in with blue lobelias and I think heucheras, along with petunias, alyssum, and whatever else the garden centers happened to be selling. Unfortunately, a very fine musk rose flourished and has reached well into her bedroom windows on the second floor, and an admirable pink honeysuckle has defied all law and reason and settled in lavishly on an iron railing she installed for it several years ago. Rammed up against the iron spindles are perhaps two dozen sorts of perennials, some of which (including the white campanulas) are trying to spread, while others gallantly hold on as long as breath holds out.

Where the produce of two hundred packs of seed, growing madly in the basement, is supposed to be planted in this garden, nobody knows.

This is an extreme case, of course, of the affliction common to almost all gardeners, and I mention it to make everybody feel much better. Most of us, after all, merely have to wander about the garden holding a new rosebush, wondering if it could not perhaps be tucked in between the hollyhock and the peony, since there is a good ten inches there, and beyond doubt the hollyhock can be tied up a little and pulled to the left. We do not, most of us, wonder where to plant an additional thousand seedlings raised in the basement in a twenty-foot garden already jammed beyond hope.

My friend, as I say, does not seem to suffer much. She is tremendously busy throughout the year, and has mastered the fine art of the scalpel, opening little slits here and there for one more plant, and she has become expert at last rites for the dying. On the whole, she is happier than she was before this madness set in. We who like her, however, are in some distress about where it will all end.

Still, as her friends tend to comfort one another when her name comes up, she's in better shape than if she took up raising cattle—a thing that mercifully has not yet occurred to her.

—from *One Man's Garden*, 1992

The Secret of
Planting a Garden

BY HELEN DILLON

My attempt at the impossible is to reconcile the collector's instinct with the desire to make a garden that is pleasant to be in, even if you don't know the name of a single plant. This is a challenging task because a collector's garden is all too frequently a cabinet of curiosities, a glorious confection of plants, some planted in splendid isolation as befits their rarity, most dotted about anywhere there is a gap. Squads of smart labels in regimented rows embellish the flower beds. As you can imagine, this approach does not lead to an atmosphere of serenity.

All gardeners are collectors to a certain extent. For some, it may be all things variegated: The sight of a leaf striped in white, splashed in cream, or ever so slightly mottled in yellow brings immoderate excitement. Others are lured by alpine plants, and the more challenging they are to grow, the better. Collectors may have the urge to own every known species and cultivar in a single genus, and then to discuss the minute differences thereof with like-minded addicts. Or perhaps they simply fall in love with Shirley poppies and from then on want each and every poppy, from Himalayan blue poppies (*Meconopsis* species) and flamboyant Orientals (*Papaver orientale*) right down to the Welsh poppy (*Meconopsis cambrica*)—charm itself, but a true weed at heart.

For the irrepressible collector the thrill is threefold. You learn about a plant—by reading about it, seeing it in somebody else's garden, or listening to the gardening cognoscenti discussing it. Then ensues the chase, with attendant excitement. And finally the moment of acquisition. Bliss.

The collector's garden may thus contain an astonishing assortment of bulbs, herbaceous perennials, trees, shrubs, annuals, biennials, and roses (old-fashioned or otherwise). To organize this array of plants—remembering the soil and light requirements, aspect, season of bloom, height, spread, and color of each—is more difficult than a jigsaw puzzle, because no sooner do you finish a section than the pieces move off of their own accord. And the best-laid plans are often confounded by plants imbued with such uncontrollable wanderlust that they have no intention of staying where you put them in the first place.

Some sort of order needs to be imposed on this vast accumulation. The principal ways of doing this are, first, to give the garden a fairly formal design that will contain exuberant plantings within a strong framework; second, to group plants according to their cultural need, creating special areas for those with particular requirements, such as alpines, lime haters, shade lovers, or plants needing a sheltered spot; and third, to group plants by color.

I feel emphatically that a formal design, on however modest a scale, allows the collecting spirit free rein. You can get away with placing umpteen plants higgledy-piggledy provided they are contained within strict, architectural lines.

Even if a plant is the only known example in Ireland, if all it does is lead a miserable existence in a muddy yogurt container (along with several hundred similar victims nearby), I'd rather not have it. I not only want the plant to flower and fruit and glow with health as it would in the wild, I want to make it look comfortable in a garden setting.

To combat the threat of garden chaos, a collector not only needs to be passionate about something, but also professional and methodical. My garden in Dublin was started in 1972. I was then at the delirious beginner's stage — whenever I saw a plant, my motto was "Buy it and see." After four years, I became a bit more organized, and since 1976, records have been kept of every plant added to the garden, with a note indicating whence it came. It makes soul-searching reading: the plants that die; those given up because they were not worth growing; the one-and-the-same plant acquired under no less than four different names; the twenty-three different alliums of which few survived onion neck rot; and the ravishing plants I have fallen for over and over again, such as *Paraquilegia anemonoïdes* (Zone 5) — plants I'm determined, just once, to grow well. The records are in a box I hesitate to open, so full is it of memories of gardeners and their gardens.

Visitors assume that one night, in a flash of creativity, I designed this garden. Not so. My method is to wait until some part of it annoys me and then take action. I'm usually satisfied with it in winter and spring, but by late summer all the mistakes show. Endless adjustments have taken place; in the paths, the shapes of beds, and, above all, in the planting. . . .

Sometimes I find myself sitting down and admiring the garden in a daze. Tunnel vision allows me to notice plants that are looking good or, contrariwise, those plants that look mysteriously unwell, which are often dug up straight away to investigate their roots. But it's only when I observe the garden with a sour, judgmental eye that inspiration arrives: Perhaps that elderly shrub could be replaced — the one I've walked past countless times without actually seeing? Perhaps that marvelous new lungwort should be propagated to make a larger patch? And what about that great vandal of a comfrey? Something must be done.

The most serious gardening I do would seem very strange to an onlooker, for it involves hours of walking round in circles, apparently doing nothing. What I'm doing is forcing myself to evaluate certain areas: criticizing the planting, noting seasonal gaps, and making imaginary moves in my head. Flowering stems are stuck into the soil and plants, still in pots, are plonked down here and there so I can consider the effect. Only during these quiet moments does a good idea suddenly occur. The odd, radical change is contemplated though rarely carried out, such as asking myself what the garden would look like if I got rid of the lawn, moved the main paths, or took out a large apple tree. Gardening is the organization of living, ever-changing organisms, and therefore must be an everlasting, ever-circling process of looking, thinking, and looking again.

—from *Garden Artistry*, 1995

Collectors

BY KEN DRUSE

If it's rare, we want it. If it's tiny and impossible to grow, we've got to have it. If it's brown, looks dead, and has black flowers, we'll kill for it.

We're collectors and little will stand in the way of bagging our quarry. We are driven by a must-have passion that singles us out from other gardeners.

The world of plant collectors is certainly one of the most exciting subcultures in horticulture, a peculiar community within the green scene. If you keep at gardening long enough, sooner or later, you'll become a collector. The plants at the local garden center just won't be enough to feed your appetite or paint the garden picture of your dreams, and the desire to possess the newest botanical curiosity will be stronger than you can stand. At that moment, you unwittingly become a member of the select collector's group.

Collectors come in various guises. . . . Some are *hunters*, part of a long tradition of people who have sought out the new and the different. Other collectors are *missionaries*, driven to save threatened plants by growing them in conservancy collections, or to spread the word about their favorites. Many collectors are impressed by a taxonomic group of plants or a particular habitat and become *specialists*. *Aesthetes* collect plants for their appearance and value in garden designs.

Though the psychology probably has much in common with that of other collectors—the antique-car connoisseurs and philatelists more than the tag-sale junkies who bring home anything and everything—there is something more here: commitment. Plants are among the highest-maintenance collectibles. But gardeners have a need to nurture, and in collectors, this need is especially keen, because very often, the more rare and odd their charges, the tougher it is to keep them happy, or even alive. . . .

Unlike precious antiques, our obsessions reproduce, so their status as one-of-a-kind rarities may be fleeting. Imagine if an emerald could, with the help of guiding hands, be cloned into an endless number of like progeny. That can be the case with a rare plant. Sometimes the process is arduous, but in most situations, rare plants have the same biological imperative to reproduce as any other living thing.

Some people collect just for the joy of acquisition. The thinking goes, if it looks good and you don't have it, get it. Accumulating is not collecting, although often, we get so wrapped up in the garage-sale mentality that we will purchase nearly anything just in case, someday, we may want it. One collector I know has an antidote for such binges. He won't grow any plant he hasn't seen. He needs to know in advance that it will reward his time and effort.

To others, there is a great thrill in being the first on the block, in the neighborhood, state, country, world, to possess a botanical rarity—no matter what it looks like.

—from *The Collector's Garden*, 1996

"Not a Place to Be Happy In"

BY ELIZABETH VON ARNIM

I have been much afflicted again lately by visitors—not stray callers to be got rid of after a due administration of tea and things you are sorry afterwards that you said, but people staying in the house and not to be got rid of at all. All June was lost to me in this way, and it was from first to last a radiant month of heat and beauty; but a garden where you meet the people you saw at break- fast, and will see again at lunch and dinner, is not a place to be happy in. Besides, they had a knack of finding out my favourite seats and lounging in them just when I longed to lounge myself; and they took books out of the library with them, and left them face downwards on the seats all night to get well drenched with dew, though they might have known that what is meat for roses is poison for books; and they gave me to understand that if they had had the arranging of the garden it would have been finished long ago—whereas I don't believe a garden ever is finished. They have all gone now, thank heaven, except one, so that I have a little breathing space before others begin to arrive. It seems that the place interests people, and that there is a sort of novelty in staying in such a deserted corner of the world, for they were in a perpetual state of mild amusement at being here at all.

—from *The Solitary Summer*, 1899

Down and Dirty

BY CYNTHIA KLING

"I'm worried about your buddleia," I said, looking at the rather shady spot my friend had chosen for this sun worshipper.

"The buddleia," he said, carefully correcting my Latin (erroneously) by adding a long "u" and a couple more syllables, "will get plenty of sun there."

As we continued the tour of my friend's garden, I silently catalogued a few other questionable practices: convolvulus creeping down the rhododendron and possibly choking the stem; the compost pile, heavy with green and light on brown, and expensive cocoa bean mulch, which is said to cause mildew, all around his phlox. He went on at some length about how many of his annuals he'd started from seed, and how he'd grown his floriferous fairy roses from cuttings.

I drove back to my house and gardened with renewed vigor for the rest of the afternoon. We wouldn't know who was the better gardener until the end of the summer, when he'd come over for a visit and we'd compare—silently and secretly, of course, but ferociously.

People who don't really understand gardening think of it as a patrician and benign hobby. That couldn't be further from the truth. To serious gardeners, it's blood sport.

I grew up in the Olympic Village of gardening, blue-blood Philadelphia, where matrons kept their husbands (and teams of gardeners, if there was any money left in the family trust) slaving all year in basements and greenhouses to get ready for the annual Philadelphia Flower Show. In March, when photographers descended on the show, everyone was all smiles. That's because we were taught to keep our gardening feuds private. But that did not mean that they were necessarily genteel. When I was 14, there was a scandal when Mrs. R.—who was both a sloppy gardener and a drinker—finally got so fed up with the blue-ribbon-toting Mrs. P. that in the dark parking lot of the Philadelphia Cricket Club, after a cocktail party, of course, she yanked her frosted-blond hairpiece off.

Gardeners rarely brawl, but they cheat whenever they can (what do you think fertilizer is for?) and lie every time someone comes over to visit. (There isn't a plant alive that wasn't better last month or last week. Recently, my neighbor actually said, "My Icelandic poppies were more beautiful five minutes ago, but I just watered them.") This is all fair game in the bragging end of the sport.

Newspapers are always writing about the fact that gardening is the fastest-growing hobby in America; at last, the baby boomers have found an appropriate pastime. Aside from the pleasures of lying, cheating and bragging, did you ever wonder why we do it?

I didn't actually start out as a fierce competitor. I began gardening when my first husband wandered off with another woman. I was left without much of a social life (jilted brides, like recently axed executives, are shunned on the dinner-party circuit). I did get a tiny apartment with a sunny terrace.

When your marriage falls apart, you feel as if everything that everyone told you about life is suddenly suspect. I stopped watching the higher forms of life, which confused me, and went to cosmos, marigolds and pansies. Plants, unlike people, are straightforward. Stick a clematis in a sunny spot with its roots shaded and it will reward you for years. Too much sun too close to its roots and it won't chase around, have affairs or go off to Esalen. It'll just keel over and die.

Three years later I'd found husband No. 2, and we bought a small cottage up on the Hudson River. In my backyard garden, my Philadelphia genes began to reassert themselves. Yet, like many of my compatriots, I'm a child of the 60's and a former leftist. Twenty years ago on the barricades and even today we eschew obvious signs of consumption.

But that doesn't mean we aren't as socially competitive as our parents; we're just a little sneakier about it. You won't find us at the garden center loading up on sod. No one I know would ever waste time cultivating a Chrysler Imperial, Dolly Parton or Betty Prior rose—too common, too easy, they bloom for too long. No, my generation had to go back to Charles de Mills, Frühlingsgold, the City of York—fusty antiques that bloom for about 20 minutes before turning back into a prickly tangle of ungainly green.

The plants we lust after are hard to find and expensive—and, I confess, they double as social-climbing tools. A few years ago I befriended the snootiest, most aristocratic publisher in New York by walking around his potagerie with him, commenting on some of his rarer specimens: How superb the figs look—how do you get them to grow in Zone 5? Only one gardener on staff—remarkable. Blah, blah, blah.

It may all seem a little over the top, and I agree it probably is. But compared with what? An old gardening book of mine says a French family went so far as to fertilize its roses with the unwanted babies of young maidens. For us, at least it's only money and energy that we're plowing into our plots.

—from *The New York Times Magazine*, August 31, 1997

Gapers and Crouchers

BY MIRABEL OSLER

Garden visitors divide into two sorts: the Gapers and the Crouchers. Each sees a garden differently. The former throw back their heads, sniff the air and open up their sensual vents, while continually altering their focus. They come to bask, and to leave rekindled. The Crouchers, on the other hand, progress through a garden (theirs or someone else's) with tunnel vision and a permanent stoop. When finally they leave the premises they have in their hands a list of accurately named plants—their booty—to be followed up at home with a search in the invaluable Royal Horticultural Society's *Plant Finder* for nurseries to supply each plant. But what they miss! They enter a garden with knees bent, specs on, and never, not for one moment, do they walk erect, take deep breaths, sense the atmosphere, assess the prevailing mood, absorb the overall quality, or respond to its impulse. Competitive and acquisitive, they move blindfolded along paths, never "seeing" the garden, merely flexing their botanical muscles.

I sigh when a Croucher comes here. It doesn't happen

often because my garden is a dead loss, it's not a place of rare delights. But my buoyancy goes limp, particularly when they say threateningly: "Can I come and see what you've got that I haven't?" ("Not a thing, not a thing," I murmur as an aside.) Inevitably he or she is going to leave here disappointed. The first thing they do is to start dropping names, the Latin ones, to prove to me that they know their onions. But it's wasted on me. I wouldn't even know if they are right or wrong, but I do know that I'm to be quizzed on "Which one?," "Surely not?," "Can you really grow this here?" (A Winter's bark, *Drimys winteri*. No, the answer is, I can't. It died last summer.) They move along the path doing what I call the Vincent Square shuffle. This needs an explanation. Vincent Square is where the Royal Horticultural Shows take place. They are oases of wonder in the heart of London and they draw devotees from far and wide. Their seasonal exhibitions are places of floral virtuosity; here we can pause with myopic stance and not be thought batty. Plants are on display here that you would die for. Instead of having a watering mouth—as I do when standing in front of market stalls in France—my eyes water, from boundless admiration and a hopeless longing doomed to be unrequited. Oh, to have such unbelievably beautiful works of floral art in the garden. To have such peerless blossoms; to have one such ravishing plant from among this throng. I defy anyone to leave Vincent Square not walking on air. Trails of us return homewards enveloped in an aura of scent and colour, and with a sweetness in our souls that wasn't there when we left.

When Crouchers come here and dampen my spirit by performing the Vincent Square shuffle, I know for certain that we are two different sorts of gardener, each seeing the place through subjective eyes; they'll leave here not having picked up the quintessence of what I'm struggling to achieve. On an autumn day recently, a Croucher walked through the garden so intent on the ground that she never noticed her reflection in my mirrors, progressing at the same pace alongside her. "No dahlias!" she cried in dismay. Well—no, actually, though it hadn't occurred to me. Since then, having seen her garden, I understand. Her garden was exploding with dahlias and begonias. She'd come hoping to find in mine unsuspected treasures that she hadn't known about. People like this return home unaware of my attitude to the whole complexity of gardening; unable even to see what has worked for me and what hasn't. Far too intent on the lexicon for their personal "plant finder," they restrain their chagrin and never come here again.

We are so out of kilter that I become downcast and feel more and more protective towards my garden; the visitor is condemning it as a failure and I'm overcome by a kind of Prince Charles plant empathy bordering on lunacy. "There, there," I say. "I love you." Even so, I've many friends among the Crouchers, and all the time I'm writing this I know that we desperately need and rely on them. They are genuine Plants People; they are as vital to our gardens as rain, because it's through them that the variety of our gardens has grown.

So with a certain remorse for what I've just written, I do make a mental genuflection to the Crouchers and Great Collectors. After all, it was Captain Francis Winter—one of Drake's men—who in 1575 was responsible for the discovery of my deceased and much-lamented *Drimys winteri*.

These two ways of looking at a garden—the Crouchers and the Gapers—were made most apparent to me when, on a humid and stifling day in August, I visited a friend's town garden, jammed with spectacular trees underplanted with spring bulbs but then, in midsummer, verdant with ferns. Ferns of every sort, rare and outlandish, sculptured and fretted, were growing from well-watered leaf mould. As the gardener named each one in a continuous litany, while he progressed doubled up, I was able to follow his bottom, free to absorb the jungly illusion of the tree canopy overhead and the transforming quality of the green luminosity. The dappling of light, the steaming poultice underfoot and the tropical atmosphere clinging to my skin held me enthralled. Latin names? The minute variety of scrolling leaves, identified by my friend one after the other, had no power over me. I was imagining gaudy butterflies and red-whiskered bulbuls glimpsed through the clammy foliage. It was an experience I shall never forget, but I rather think my host imagined that I left with a totally different imprint.

Crouchers move through a garden at a stoop: naming, gasping, hooraying, admiring or coveting plants; Gapers saunter, smiling or sighing at what they find, succumbing to an intangible beatitude that takes them for a brief escape into another dimension. Both sorts of gardener are besotted; both get their hands dirty, think and talk gardening; but on the threshold of another's garden, each uses a different set of whiskers.

—from *A Breath from Elsewhere*, 1997

The Unbehooved Gardener

BY JULIAN MEADE

Today I was plowing faithfully through a horticultural tome when I came to a chapter which began thus, "If you would have a really successful garden, it behooves you—"

The hell it does. My garden is one place in the world where I am not behooved. I know it behooves me to dig up every clump of chrysanthemums I possess, because chrysanthemums like a fresh start each year if they are to be really fine. Yes, I know that—but a more slipshod method suits me better. I break a slip of every variety I like and give it a good send-off, pinch it back, water it and feed it. But a lot of the old clumps can be discarded or they can stay where they are and they won't be so insignificant at that.

The more I hear of Horticulture, the more I like plain gardening. There was an argument here today as to how we should pronounce Heuchera, a miserable cognomen for a good perennial whose racemes of pink, rose, white blossoms, airy little bell-shaped blooms on slender stems, look so cheerful with Dutch iris and sweet William and any of their many affinities. My dictionary says Heu'-ker-ah but why say anything like that about a flower with the respectable name of coral-bells? (Leave out the white variety, which isn't a heart-breaking act, and that name is accurate as well as pleasant.)

Another visitor—and this is no prevarication—insisted that I should know a beautiful new iris called "Cystitis." I felt sure the lady was wrong but she was impressively certain. I kept a straight face till she left and then rushed to Webster to see if I wasn't right in thinking she confused urology with horticulture. For once, Webster was with me! Poor lady! She was the very soul of propriety. I'd love to see her when she discovers her error.

Many fine flowers are cursed with atrocious names. I'd just as soon call an iris "Cystitis" as to call it a name inspired by some gas-bag politician or some movie queen who wouldn't know her namesake's pistil from its stamens.

Flowers we like to grow should have names that please us and it's a joy to find them honoring men and women who have excelled in the world of gardens. Weeds, on the other hand, should have names we loathe, so we can go about their destruction with more zest and vim. The process of weeding is more sanative if you name the pests after your own special enemies and pet abominations. Don't bother to learn whether your new intruder is pigweed or horse nettle. Just christen it in honor of some neighbor whom you find difficult to "love as thyself" and, while abolishing it, you also may vent your spleen.

—from *Bouquets and Bitters*, 1940

from the Introduction to
Onward and Upward
in the Garden

BY E. B. WHITE

When Miss Gertrude Jekyll, the famous English woman who opened up a whole new vista of gardening for Victorian England, prepared herself to work in her gardens, she pulled on a pair of Army boots and tied on an apron fitted with great pockets for her tools. Unlike Miss Jekyll, my wife had no garden clothes and never dressed for gardening. When she paid a call on her perennial borders or her cutting bed or her rose garden, she was not dressed for the part—she was simply a spur-of-the-moment escapee from the house and, in the early years, from the job of editing manuscripts. Her Army boots were likely to be Ferragamo shoes, and she wore no apron. I seldom saw her *prepare* for gardening, she merely wandered out into the cold and the wet, into the sun and the warmth, wearing whatever she had put on that morning. Once she was drawn into the fray, once involved in transplanting or weeding or thinning or pulling deadheads, she forgot all else; her clothes had to take things as they came. I, who was the animal husbandryman on the place, in blue jeans and an old shirt, used to marvel at how unhesitatingly she would kneel in the dirt and begin grubbing about, garbed in a spotless cotton dress or a handsome tweed skirt and jacket. She simply refused to dress *down* to a garden: she moved in elegantly and walked among her flowers as she walked among her friends—nicely dressed, perfectly poised. If when she arrived back indoors the Ferragamos were encased in muck, she kicked them off. If the tweed suit was a mess, she sent it to the cleaner's.

The only moment in the year when she actually got herself up for gardening was on the day in the fall that she had selected, in advance, for the laying out of the spring bulb garden—a crucial operation, carefully charted and full of witchcraft. The morning often turned out to be raw and overcast, with a searching wind off the water—an easterly that finds its way quickly to your bones. The bad weather did not deter Katharine: the hour had struck, the strategy of spring must be worked out according to plan. This particular bulb garden, with its many varieties of tulips, daffodils, narcissi, hyacinths, and other spring blooms, was a sort of double-duty affair. It must provide a bright mass of color in May, and it must also serve as a source of supply—flowers could be stolen from it for the building of experimental centerpieces.

Armed with a diagram and a clipboard, Katharine would get into a shabby old Brooks raincoat much too long for her, put on a little round wool hat, pull on a pair of overshoes, and proceed to the director's chair—a folding canvas thing—that had been placed for her at the edge of the plot. There she would sit, hour after hour, in the wind and the weather, while Henry Allen produced dozens of brown paper packages of new bulbs and a basketful of old ones, ready for the intricate interment. As the years went by and age overtook her, there was something comical yet touching in her bedraggled appearance on this awesome occasion —the small, hunched-over figure, her studied absorption in the implausible notion that there would be yet another spring, oblivious to the ending of her own days, which she knew perfectly well was near at hand, sitting there with her detailed chart under those dark skies in the dying October, calmly plotting the resurrection.

—from *Onward and Upward in the Garden*, 1979

DESIGN IN THE GARDEN

Knowing how to grow things is important if
you want to make a garden, but not as important as people make out; it's knowing
where to put them that matters.

—*MARY KEEN, 1987*

In Search of Style

BY RUSSELL PAGE

Garden-making, like gardening itself, concerns the relationship of the human being to his natural surroundings. The idiom has changed from place to place and from one period to another, whether we consider the smallest medieval herb garden, a tiny formal pattern set against the curtain wall of a fortified castle, or the enormous perspectives which Le Nôtre cut symmetrically through the gentle slopes and forests of the Ile de France. Occasionally gardens have been used for a wider and deeper intention. A handful of men working within the Zen sect of Buddhism created gardens in fifteenth-century Japan which were, and still are, far more than merely an aesthetic expression. And what is left of the earlier Mogul gardens in India suggests that their makers were acquainted with what lay behind the flowering of the Sufi movement in High Asia and so sought to add further dimensions to their garden scenes.

I know that I cannot make anything new. To make a garden is to organise all the elements present and add fresh ones, but first of all, I must absorb as best I can all that I see, the sky and the skyline, the soil, the colour of the grass and the shape and nature of the trees. Each half-mile of countryside has its own nature and every few yards is a reinterpretation. Each stone where it lies says something of the earth's underlying structure; and the plants growing there, whether native or exotic, will indicate the vegetable chemistry of that one place.

Such things show the limitations of a site and limitations imply possibilities. A problem is a challenge. I cannot remember a completely characterless site though, for example, a walled rectangle of sandy earth in the Nile Valley with not a tree visible would seem to qualify as such. So would a stretch of flat sugar-beet field in the industrial North of France with pylons of high tension wires standing across a bleak landscape relieved only by factory chimneys on the horizon. Even so you can always turn to something for a starting point. In the first (an actual case) the hot blue sky, cloudless all the year round, offered an easy answer— shade. A garden should be devised through which one would always walk in shade. Shade implied trees. A mango grove became the main theme of the garden and all its parts and details were subjected to the over-riding theme. For another reason trees, too, were the answer in the second case: not for shade, but to bring an illusion of wilder country into a man-spoilt landscape. Time was a factor here. The house was ugly and there was little labour available for the upkeep of a garden. I chose to plant young birch trees, and now, twenty years later, the house is veiled in a haze of birches light enough not to steal the sun, while their branches and the haphazard colonnade of their silvered trunks hide the ugly view.

Unlike painting or sculpture or buildings a garden grows. Its appearance changes—plants mature, some in six weeks, some in six hundred years. There are few gardens that can be left alone. A few years of neglect and only the skeleton of a garden can be traced—the modelling of the ground perhaps, walls or steps, a pool, the massing of trees. Japanese artists working with a few stones and sand four hundred years ago achieved strangely lasting compositions. However there, too, but for the hands that have piously raked the white sand into patterns and controlled the spread of moss and lichens, little would remain.

We live under an accumulation of periods and styles and cultures. The variations of artistic expression over the whole world for the last four thousand years are available, a vast store of information making a vast confusion. Architecture has found a way out through functionalism and has largely become applied and often splendid engineering. Painters and sculptors, struggling to free themselves from a top-heavy load, have experimented with association-patterns dug from the different layers of their consciousness.

I think that creative gardening need not suffer from these, the results of a changing, if not a disintegrating culture. It can begin from another point. A seed, a plant, a tree must each obey the laws of its nature. Any serious interference with these and it must die. It will only grow and thrive when the conditions for it are approximately right. If you wish to make anything grow you must understand it, and understand it in a very real sense. "Green fingers" are a fact, and a mystery only to the unpractised. But green fingers are the extensions of a verdant heart. A good garden cannot be made by somebody who has not developed the capacity to know and to love growing things.

Such intangibilities are facts and a whole new world waits to be explored. Any starting point will do — a seedling in a three-inch flower-pot to grow into a magic beanstalk up which we can climb to open a gate into another aspect of this world, just this world which lies around us and in which we move perhaps quite unsuspecting of its possibilities.

Processes have always given me more satisfaction than results. Perhaps this is peculiarly English and may explain our national affection for a pursuit which is always changing: growth and decay, the swing of the seasons, our inconstant weather speeding or retarding the development of a tree or the flowering and seeding of a plant. English gardens seem to be always in flux. The fugitive pleasures which gardening affords seem to be enhanced for us by a subtle and deliberate disorder that softens the emphasis of a straight line and never allows the garden to appear static or achieved. A climate which favours the growing of plants from all over the world must have contributed to the fact that the English have been pioneers in the breeding and selection of plants and domestic animals. A native dislike for a coldly logical formulation, or the half termination of a spoken phrase, suggests that a subject need never be exhausted; it is always in growth; there is always room and time for further trial and adaptation.

—from *The Education of a Gardener,* 1962

from The Epistle to Burlington

BY ALEXANDER POPE

To build, to plant, whatever you intend,
To rear the Column, or the Arch to bend,
To swell the Terras, or to sink the Grot;
In all, let Nature never be forgot.
But treat the Goddess like a modest fair,
Nor over-dress, nor leave her wholly bare;
Let not each beauty ev'ry where be spy'd,
Where half the skill is decently to hide.
He gains all points, who pleasingly confounds,
Surprizes, varies, and conceals the Bounds.

Consult the Genius of the Place in all;
That tells the Waters or to rise, or fall,
Or helps th' ambitious Hill the heav'n to scale,
Or scoops in circling theatres the Vale,
Calls in the Country, catches opening glades,
Joins willing woods, and varies shades from shades,
Now breaks or now directs, th' intending Lines;
Paints as you plant, and, as you work, designs.

—1731

Plants Do Not
a Garden Make

BY GERTRUDE JEKYLL

I am strongly of the opinion that the possession of a quantity of plants, however good the plants may be themselves and however ample their number, does not make a garden; it only makes a *collection*. Having got the plants, the great thing is to use them with careful selection and definite intention. Merely having them, or having them planted unassorted in garden spaces, is only like having a box of paints from the best colourman, or, to go one step further, it is like having portions of these paints set out upon a palette. This does not constitute a picture; and it seems to me that the duty we owe to our gardens and to our own bettering in our gardens is so to use the plants that they shall form beautiful pictures; and that, while delighting our eyes they should be always training those eyes to a more exalted criticism; to a state of mind and artistic conscience that will not tolerate bad or careless combination or any sort of misuse of plants, but in which it becomes a point of honour to be always striving for the best. It is just in the way it is done that lies the whole difference between commonplace gardening and gardening that may rightly claim to rank as a fine art. Given the same space of ground and the same material, they may either be fashioned into a dream of beauty . . . or they may be so misused that everything is jarring and displeasing. To learn how to perceive the difference and how to do right is to apprehend gardening as a fine art.

—from *Wood and Garden,* 1899

A Question of Design

BY BEVERLEY NICHOLS

To be asked to design other people's gardens is flattering, particularly when the people who seek advice have understood what one has been trying to do in one's own garden and have appreciated one's basic principles — the elimination of squares and triangles, the flow of melodic lines, the vital part played by water, the many *trompe l'oeil* devices which double the area, the use of colour, and especially of coloured foliage. And I can imagine no more pleasing profession than that of the landscape gardener — always providing that one's employer was a millionaire of a docile temperament, who would guarantee to leave the country for at least three years while one was getting on with the job, and would give an undertaking, on his return, to refrain from changing the disposition of a single leaf. In these days such patrons are few and far between, so that one wonders whether the landscape gardener has much of a future. However, it is his present that here concerns me, the trials and tribulations of his job as he goes about his daily business. These I can best describe by an account of my own experiences, on the few occasions when I have tried to help people "on a business basis."

We will call the first lady Mrs. Lewis. She was a blonde of about thirty-five, with a buxom figure, a turned-up nose, and immense blue eyes, which regarded the world with evident complacency. She inhabited a large neo-Tudor house some ten miles west of London, whither I was bidden to tea. Her husband, who was not at home, was "something in the city"—a very affluent something, judging by the Italian Primitives in the hall. In spite of the fact that she had apparently just emerged from a bath of Lanvin's Arpège, and omitted to dry herself, she was rather nice. She was certainly all eagerness to make a garden. Tea had scarcely been served, with a great clatter of neo-Georgian silver, before she had sprung to her feet and was conducting me to the terrace.

"If only," she cried, "if only you could make me something beautiful out of this!"

Before us stretched a bleak square of about two acres, entirely surrounded by a new brick wall about eight feet high. Behind this wall, at irregular intervals, loomed the roofs of her neighbours' houses, which were comparatively small, and clustered around like poor relations. The main feature of the "garden" was a rockery of singular repulsiveness, jutting out from a geometrical complex of triangular rose beds. (I suspected, rightly, that she had designed it herself.) In the distance was a tennis court entirely surrounded, on all four sides, by asparagus beds.

"Well," I said with feigned brightness, "we can but try."

"And where do I begin?" she demanded. "That is what baffles me. What must I do to *begin* with?"

The answer to this question was simple, but difficult to phrase politely. What Mrs. Lewis must do to begin with was to go away, immediately, and as far as possible. It is quite impossible to design anything of any value with people breathing down one's neck. One needs total solitude to arrange even a bunch of flowers.

But how to explain this to Mrs. Lewis?

"In your book," she said, "you wrote that you always began with water. Now, where shall we put our water?"

"That depends on what sort of water you want—whether it's merely to be part of the design—just a patch of silver—or whether you want to grow things in it. Lilies, for instance."

"I must have masses and *masses* of lilies!"

"In that case . . ."

But she was not listening. "I thought . . . over there. By the wall."

Her hand swept to the right, to a patch of lawn that was in deep shade.

"I'm afraid that wouldn't do."

"Not *do*? Why?"

"Because if you want water-lilies they must be in full sunlight."

"*All* water-lilies?"

"All that will grow in this country."

"Are you sure?"

"Quite sure."

"Well, of course, if you say so." She frowned. "Then what do you suggest?"

"I would make a circular pool bang in the middle of the lawn and just see what happens. As soon as it's in being, it'll start to suggest things." I pointed ahead to a distance of about thirty yards. "Out there, for instance, where you've put the deck chairs and the parasols."

"That would be *quite* impossible."

"Why?"

"Because that's where Mr. Lewis likes to do his sunbathing."

"But couldn't he sunbathe by the lily-pool?"

"I don't think he'd care for it," she observed. "I don't think you know Mr. Lewis."

She was well aware that I did not know Mr. Lewis.

"If there's a mosquito within a hundred miles," she continued, "it goes straight for Mr. Lewis. So we'll have to think of somewhere else, shan't we?"

"There doesn't seem to be anywhere else — except the tennis court."

"You're not suggesting that we should put the pool in the tennis court?"

"No. But we might do away with the tennis court altogether."

"Do *away* with it? But it's only just been put in!"

"Then couldn't we screen it off?"

"How?"

"Well . . . we could plant groups of conifers round it. And we could mask all that ugly wire-netting with climbing roses, and honeysuckles, and that sort of thing."

She shook her head energetically. "I doubt whether that would appeal to Mr. Lewis. In fact, I'm sure it wouldn't. You see, he takes his tennis very seriously. He's having lessons from a professional. And somehow . . . roses and honeysuckles . . . and *professional* tennis . . . they don't seem to go together."

"Perhaps not. All the same, if you really want a lily-pool . . ."

"I can't *live* without a lily-pool!"

I scanned the horizon. In the furthest corner there was an old curved wall that looked as though it night be concealing some little secret garden. One might contrive something quite pleasing there, provided that there was enough sunlight. It wouldn't be ideal but it would be better than nothing.

So I said to Mrs. Lewis, "What goes on behind that wall?"

"Nothing. Just a lot of rubbish heaps. Why?"

"Couldn't we put the water garden in *there*? And add to the height of the wall, and make a rather pretty path—in old red brick—leading up to it?" For the first time in this frustrating conversation, I began to feel a spark of enthusiasm. "We might find a pair of old Italian gates, in wrought iron. And we could have a fountain. And the whole thing could be self-contained, with a lovely element of surprise. And if you take my advice, you'd keep everything pure white. Lilies, white foxgloves, white roses, clusters of white phlox, hostas with white-and-green leaves . . ."

And then I caught her eye. She was staring at me with the sort of expression that a nurse in a mental hospital might reserve for a patient who, though not violent, was exceptionally tiresome.

She spoke slowly and very clearly, with a great deal of lip movement, as though addressing a deaf-mute. "Mr. Nichols, I don't think you quite understand the situation. You see, I have two small children." She paused and then added—her lips working overtime—"Very Small Children."

She made them sound like midgets.

"Yes?"

"I *have* to think of them."

I felt like saying, "So what?" If you are a millionairess, equipped with midgets, you probably think of very little else.

"Of course."

"You understand?"

I did not understand at all. "I'm afraid . . ."

She interrupted me with a tinkling laugh. "It's easy to see you're a bachelor!" She was still very friendly. She laid a gentle hand on my arm. "If *you* had two Very Small Children, would you like to think of them Out There"—she pointed, as though to immense distances—"out of sight, out of sound?"

At last I thought I understood. "I don't think they'd do much harm."

"*Do* much harm?" She removed her hand abruptly. "But what about *them*?"

"Oh, I see. You mean, they might fall in?"

"That is precisely what I mean."

"But that wouldn't matter at all," I said brightly. "The water need be only eighteen inches deep." Since she made no comment I continued. "In fact, there are several lilies which do quite well in only fifteen inches. Of course, you'd have to top the pool up in the summer but I imagine that would present no problems?"

She achieved a smile, with a great effort. "I'm afraid," she said, "we seem to be talking a different language. I mean—the very idea—I should never have a moment's peace." Another heroic smile. "Well, that would seem to be the end of our little pool, wouldn't it?"

I made a last effort. "Have you thought about the entrance?"

"What about the entrance?"

"Well, you have a very large courtyard. If it were treated formally . . ."

She shook her head with great emphasis. "That would be *out* of the question. The cars!"

"What cars?"

"Mr. Lewis has three cars, in *constant* use. He *has* to."

"But I thought I saw two quite substantial garages?"

She ignored the interruption. "Apart from that he does a great deal of entertaining. He *has* to."

"But couldn't his guests park in the road?"

Her only answer was a pitying smile.

Out of politeness, she asked me to stay for another half-hour, and conducted me round the rest of the garden. And out of politeness I continued to make suggestions, knowing full well that they would all be flatly rejected. Remove two of the asparagus beds? Impossible! If there was one thing that Mr. Lewis really doted on, it was his asparagus. Block out the surrounding houses with screens of conifers? But they would take so long to grow, and it would hardly be neighborly, would it? Mr. Lewis was held in great esteem by the neighbours. Modify the rockery? What did I mean by 'modify'? What I meant, of course, was throw the whole horrid thing on to the rubbish heap, but I could hardly say that, since Mrs. Lewis informed me that she had designed it herself.

So, after a decent interval I looked at my watch, remarked upon the lateness of the hour, and suggested that perhaps the best plan would be for me to make a rough sketch-map to send to her for her approval—an idea which she accepted with relief, as likely to get us both out of a somewhat embarrassing situation.

On the way out I met Mr. Lewis letting himself into the hall. He was quite different from what I had expected. He appeared to be younger than his wife and he looked more like a country squire than a city man. After offering me a drink, which I declined, he turned to Mrs. Lewis.

"Well, darling, everything settled?"

She smiled wanly. "One can't make a garden overnight, dear. As Mr. Nichols would be the first to tell you."

"Of course not. All the same, I bet that we shan't be long, once you get cracking." He winked at me. "Wonderful woman, my wife. Knows what she wants and usually gets it."

"All the same"—I could not resist the temptation to say this—"I gather that you have some fairly strong views yourself? About the garden, I mean?"

"Me? Good Lord, no! Leave it entirely to her. If she wants to flood the whole damned thing and turn it into a lake, God bless her! *I* shan't complain. By the way, *is* that what she wants to do?"

"I'm not quite sure." My eyes met those of Mrs. Lewis. "There's still a great deal to be discussed. And please don't bother . . . I can see myself out."

So much for Mrs. Lewis. Because I liked her, in spite of her silliness, I sent her the sketch-map. Which she acknowledged, with a very nice letter, and a large jar of caviar, the most expensive variety obtainable, and all the more delicious for being free of tax. That represents just about the sum total of the rewards I have received in the profession of landscape gardening.

—from *Garden Open Tomorrow*, 1968

Taste

BY GEOFFREY B. CHARLESWORTH

I love pretentiousness. The grand gesture. The Statement. Sometimes I feel that my own style of gardening is too diffuse, understated, diffident. There is the flamboyant eruption in May and June, of course, but everybody has that. You would have to work hard not to have a highly dramatic garden then. Spring makes its own statement, so loud and clear that the gardener seems to be only one of the instruments, not the composer. But I feel sometimes the need for a hundred feet of water flowing down stone steps as in the gardens at Chatsworth or a pagoda like Kew's. Or not even buildings; just an *allée* of pleached hornbeams or a topiary garden filled with elephants and huntsmen.

How I wish one of my ancestors had filched a marble from Athens or an obelisk from Egypt, or at least plundered enough wealth legally to hire an Italian sculptor to mold a set of lead shepherds and shepherdesses. What glitter the powerful and wealthy have left for us! Without their wickedness and greed, none of these bursts of artistic energy would have been released. Can we admire Blenheim, Versailles, or even Longwood and see only the land-scaper's art? Or the Ginkakuji in Kyoto? The statement these gardens make is a rhetoric only the blind could fail to recognize.

Do our own gardens give us away in the same manner? A single painted gnome sends out a message we think we can read and either tolerate or ridicule. If your immediate reaction is a patronizing dismissal of both gnome and owner, you had better examine very carefully your own trash-filled life. I saw a garden years ago in the west of England which was filled with gnomes, owls, verse-inscribed plaques, grotesqueries of every description placed demurely amongst the rocks and plants— a tight, well-kept little garden which was generously open to casual passers-by. The public obviously visited it and loved it. What was the significance of this extravagant statement? The message begins to elude you when you think about the person, a piece of whose soul is laid bare in front of you. Words like "tasteless" are merely buzz-words of the patronizing. Taste can only handle ideas within a local, contemporary canon; you have to know the rules before you can pass judgment on whether a particular Italian garden or a particular Medieval cloister is taste-less. We can't use such strong language about historic or exotic manifestations. To do so would be tasteless. Or pretentious? Is Mount Rushmore tasteless? Do you have to know the life history of the subject and the motive of the artist before you can use words like "tasteless" and "pretentious?"

These thoughts are not irrelevant to visitors of gardens. Some gardens came into existence to honor or flatter a man; and some gardens are comparable to a cathedral added to over many years by different people with different motives. Others display the horticultural ideas of a single mind. Our own gardens should not have to suffer such convoluted speculation in the minds of our friends and visitors. Everybody feels his own garden is unself-consciously "just a garden." Psychoanalysis on the basis of one's scree or woodland is out of place. But you can't help thinking that there must be something written there, if only you knew how to read it.

  —from *The Opinionated Gardener*, 1988

Classical or Romantic?

BY STEPHEN LACEY

I would be surprised to discover that I was the only person whose most exciting gardening moments are spent in the bath. Most keen gardeners are incurable romantics and every opportunity of drifting away into a world inhabited by stout Himalayan poppies, fat lewisias and giant marrows is greedily snatched. And where better for a prolonged and uninterrupted daydream than the bathroom? Within those tiled walls, with catalogues, seed lists and reference books at your elbow and warm soapy water rippling against your chest, imagination can run riot. Gardens become fragments of paradise. Exotic shrubs, exploding with flower and fruit, burst from every dark corner; velvet roses and sweet-scented jasmine cascade down every wall and pillar in clouds of spray; while great rivers of bulbs surge through orchard and shrubbery, cutting deep channels between trees laden with blossom.

Most memorable garden pictures, whether they are elaborate compositions or simple plant associations, have been conceived in such daydreams. They have a vague beginning, usually

115

as a blend of colours or a mixture of scents, and slowly they take shape, evolving into wild and wonderful images which often seem absurdly ambitious, daring and frivolous in design. Romantic gardeners' notebooks are crammed with messages such as "Build pagoda on site of old coal bunker" or "Turn terrace into Persian carpet." Whenever we have an idle moment, at the breakfast table, in a bus queue or on a railway station platform, these precious notes are taken out and carefully considered, and eventually a way is found to translate the images from the realms of fantasy to the realms of reality.

Sometimes an idea has to be modified for one reason or another. A pagoda is all very well but it will probably be too expensive to construct and, truth be told, might look rather incongruous in the corner of a suburban garden. What we really want is an object which is attractive and which will conjure up the fragrant riches of the east; and, of course, that bunker does have to go. Or does it? Why not just remove its roof, its wooden door and window-frames, knock it about with a sledge-hammer and leave the rest to *Rosa longicuspis* which, given a well-manured start, will soon ramble through the apertures and conceal the brickwork in a tangle of growth? In midsummer it will be smothered in deliciously scented, creamy yellow flowers, as sumptuous an oriental feast as we could hope for. . . .

Composing such garden pictures is probably the most satisfying and the most rewarding aspect of gardening. It is also the most challenging, since it requires a fusion of two sets of skills, creative and practical. Few of us possess both in equal measure which is why our attempts at artistic gardening are largely such hit or miss affairs. Either we misplace shapes and colours or we misjudge the times certain plants are in flower and the size to which they grow. I suspect the great majority of us commit both sorts of error. Autumn is certainly heralded in my garden by the lifting of numbers of plants which I have failed to integrate properly into my various schemes. The wheelbarrow is filled with clumps of yellow daylilies which finished flowering a week before the pale blue agapanthus with which they were supposed to associate, with carmine tradescantia which was not after all subdued by a gentle backcloth of pale pink geraniums, or with mounds of dejected diascia which scarcely produced a single flower in their shady position behind fountains of silver dorycnium.

Fortunately, we do not have to rely entirely on a process of trial and error. If we did, those autumn operations would be monumental. On the practical side, there are many ways of improving our chances of success. Apart from observing closely the behaviour of plants in our own garden, we can visit botanical gardens and gardens open on the National Gardens Scheme and take note of methods of cultivation, the ultimate height and width of individual plants and the conditions in which they flourish. We can refer to an enormous library of gardening books, which covers every subject from the combating of aphid attack to the raising of prize-winning parsnips, from the pruning of Chinese wisteria to the propagation of carnations and pinks. We can watch the experts on television digging small ponds, making peat gardens and planting window-boxes and hanging baskets. Advice is available in all forms and on all subjects.

In comparison, creative advice is scarce. Of course, we can collect plenty of ideas from our garden visiting. Nearly everybody's garden has some aspect of design worth noting. There are also a number of books which deal with garden design, telling us how to devise an overall plan or how to site trees and paths. But the shortage of material is apparent when we start to think about the composition of particular plant groups, once the backbone of design is completed. We have our hedges and our paths, our lawns and our flowerbeds; we have placed our trees and planned our focal points and our conceits; we have set aside an area for growing vegetables and fruit, a plot for the greenhouse and a place for the washing-line. The remaining task is to design schemes for each area of bare soil and to draw up lists of shrubs, perennials and bulbs. Where do we begin?

Classical gardeners will always start with shapes. They will see each area as an architectural problem which needs an architectural solution. An upright form at the back perhaps, slightly to the right, with a couple of large rounded shrubs in front and groups of smaller plants in the foreground; including on the left a short upright form to echo and balance the shape at the back. Maybe they want a contrast of broad leaves against narrow leaves or spikes of flowers against flat umbels; maybe they want a groundwork of small-leaved plants, above which the two vertical shapes will rise like church spires from a winter mist. Eventually, as they are making their list of plants they might spare a thought for colour and scent.

The romantic gardener's approach is entirely the reverse. Our starting-point is that hazy bathroom vision and our intention is to capture it by means of a careful selection of colours. Shapes and forms are still important considerations but they are definitely secondary ones. Each area of soil is pictured as a colour scheme and only when the colours have been decided will we begin to think about anything else.

The very best gardens are undoubtedly those which have had the benefit of both the classical and the romantic influence, for then the pitfalls of each approach—that the classical garden tends to be rigid and unexciting and the romantic garden tends to be wild and shapeless—are avoided. Sissinghurst is a prime example. It was made by Vita Sackville-West and Harold Nicolson. Vita was the romantic, the poet, the plantswoman; Harold was the classicist, the scholar, the politician. Together they fashioned the epitome of the perfect garden in which a strict linear framework is softened by exuberant and informal planting. It was not always an easy partnership for the classical and romantic temperaments do not give in to each other without a struggle, as this extract from Harold Nicolson's diary demonstrates: "In the afternoon I moon about with Vita trying to convince her that planning is an element in gardening. . . . The tragedy of the romantic temperament is that it dislikes form so much that it ignores the effect of masses. She wants to put in stuff which 'will give a lovely red colour in autumn.' I wish to put in stuff which will furnish shape to the perspective. In the end we part, not as friends."

Very few of us have the steadying influence of a classical partner to temper our activities (I am assuming that you, like me, have a romantic temperament), so we must make a special effort, at some stage in the design process, to stand back, assume the guise of classical critic and look for flaws in our schemes. Have they got substance? Are there clear architectural lines? Do the different shapes make a coherent whole? Or are they just vague and disorderly images which will look untidy at flowering and positively chaotic afterwards?

Providing we do remember to scrutinize our compositions for structural elements some time before we start planting, our preoccupation with more poetic matters should not lead us far astray. Indeed, we have some justification for treating colour as the main aspect of design. The fact is that the eye appreciates colour before it appreciates shape. Look around the room in which you are now sitting and notice how your attention is immediately drawn to the brightest colours and not to the most striking shapes. The only time that we notice shapes straightaway is when the range of colours is limited. Hence it is extremely dangerous for any garden designer to consider colour only as an afterthought because its careless use can seriously interfere with the intended picture. There are examples of such occurrences in every Chelsea Flower Show, where designers have clearly laboured painstakingly over the architectural aspects of their plans and then unwittingly destroyed their creations by the reckless use of colour. All the architectural movement advances in one direction while the bright colours (usually azaleas) compel the eye to follow a different course.

Although colour is the most important element in the romantic gardener's designs, most of us have little understanding of its nature or potential. Even if we think we have a clear impression of a particular scheme in our mind, its impact on the ground is often quite different, as colours react unexpectedly with their neighbours or are affected by changing light. Some of us have difficulty matching colours, producing harmonious pictures or handling strong hues. Others know what mood they wish to convey but are unsure which colours will properly convey it.

All these difficulties can eventually be overcome by experiment but we can save ourselves a lot of time and trouble if we are prepared to devote just a few moments to an investigation of the colour laws and a study of the principles of colour combination. If we understand the relationships between colours, we will be better able to appreciate how a harmony and a contrast is produced and what its likely impact will be, and we will be able to solve our problems systematically. Of course, there are no firm rules for the making of colour schemes—and there is certainly no guarantee of success—but there are clear principles which, if followed, will considerably improve our chances of capturing the exact image or conjuring up the exact mood which engulfed us in our bath tub.

Scent is no less potent a substance and is never far from the romantic gardener's thoughts. Because it is not visual, it is generally distributed quite carelessly through the garden and rarely becomes an integral part of a scheme, but its presence is always keenly felt and it has as dramatic an impact on our senses as colour, often more so. It is because of this that the romantic seeks to sprinkle it everywhere. Unfortunately, we know far less about scent than about colour and because it is such an unpredictable substance, we are unable to manage it with quite the same confidence. Nevertheless, we are occasionally tempted to pursue scented themes in our borders, perhaps inspired by the perfumes of old roses infused with the fruit fragrance of philadelphus or the pungent odour of rosemary seasoned with lavender and thyme. . . .

A preoccupation with colour and scent is not the only trait which distinguishes the romantic from the classical garden. The role played by plants in each garden is also entirely different. In the classical garden plants are just another ingredient in the design, no more and no less important than paths and walls, but in the romantic garden they are the very basis of and reason for the design. Romantic gardeners have a deep passion for plants for their own sake and the design of our gardens has to be flexible enough to cope with an ever-changing and ever-increasing plant population. We are unable to pass any nursery by without investigating its content and making a purchase and are the slaves of any plant catalogue which falls through the letter-box. Our gardens thus tend to comprise a very broad and diverse collection of plants, each chosen on its own merits, rather than according to the strict requirements of a preconceived plan. It is our passion for scheming and the care with which each plant is sited that saves the garden from becoming a complete hotchpotch of disconnected images.

—from *The Startling Jungle,* 1990

A Gentle Plea for Chaos

BY MIRABEL OSLER

Looking round gardens, how many of them lack that quality which adds an extra sensory dimension for the sake of orderliness? There is an antiseptic tidiness which characterizes a well-controlled gardener. And I'd go further and say that usually the gardener is male. Men seem more obsessed with order in the garden than women. They are pre-occupied with flower bed edges cut with the precision of a pre-war hair cut. Using a lethal curved blade, they chop along the grass to make it conform to their schoolboy set squares, and with a dustpan and brush they collect 1 cm of wanton grass. Or, once they hold a hedge-trimmer, within seconds they have guillotined all those tender little growths on hawthorn or honeysuckle hedges that add to the blurring and enchantment of a garden in early June.

The very soul of a garden is shrivelled by zealous regimentation. Off with their heads go the ferns, ladies' mantles or crane's bill. A mania for neatness, a lust for conformity and away goes atmosphere and sensuality. What is left? Earth between plants; the dreaded tedium of clumps of colour with earth between. So the garden is reduced to merely a place of plants. Step — one, two. Stop — one, two; look down (no need ever to look up for there is no mystery ahead to draw you on), look down at each plant. Individually each is sublime undoubtedly. For a plantsman this is heaven. But where is lure? And where, alas, is seduction and gooseflesh on the arms?

There is a place for precision, naturally. Architectural lines such as those from hedges, walls, paths or topiary are the bones of a garden. But it is the artist who then allows for dishevelment and abandonment to evolve. People say gardening is the one occupation over which they have control. Fine. But why over-indulge? Control is vital for the original design and form; and a ruthless strength of mind is essential when you have planted some hideous thing you lack the courage to demolish. But there is a point when your steadying hand should be lifted and a bit of native vitality can be allowed to take over.

One of the small delights of gardening, undramatic but recurring, is when phlox or columbines seed themselves in unplanned places. When trickles of creeping jenny soften stony outlines or Welsh poppies cram a corner with their brilliant cadmium yellow alongside the deep blue spires of Jacob's ladder all arbitrarily seeding themselves like coloured smells about the place.

Cottage gardens used to have this quality. By their naturally evolved planting, brought about by the necessity of growing herbs and fruit trees, cabbages and gooseberries, amongst them there would be hollyhocks and honesty, campanulas and pinks. How rare now to see a real cottage garden. It is far more difficult to achieve than a contrived garden. It requires intuition, a genius for letting things have their heads.

In the Mediterranean areas this can still be seen. Discarded cans once used for fetta cheese, olives or salt fish, are painted blue or white and stuffed to overflowing with geraniums placed with unaffected artlessness on steps or walls, under trees or on a window sill. Old tins are planted with basil, they stand on the threshold of a house, not for culinary use because basil is a sacred plant, but for the aromatic pleasure when a sprig is picked for a departing traveller. Under a vine shading the well, are aubergines, melons, courgettes and a scatter of gaudy zinnias. An uncatalogued rose is grown for its scent near a seat where a fig tree provides shade and fruit. Common sense and unselfconsciousness have brought this about. A natural instinct inspired by practical necessity. We are too clever by half. We read too many books, we make too many notes. We lie too long in the bath planning gardens. Have we lost our impulsive faculties? Have we lost that intuitive feel for the flow and rightness of things; our awareness of the dynamics of a garden where things scatter where they please?

And this brings me to another observation which I think goes with my original longing for a little shambles here and there. For it seems that proper gardeners never sit in their gardens. Dedicated and single-minded the garden draws them into its embrace where their passions are never assuaged unless they are on their knees. But for us, the unserious, the improper people, who plant and drift, who prune and amble, we fritter away little dollops of time in sitting about our gardens. Benches for sunrise, seats for contemplation, resting perches for the pure sublimity of smelling the evening air or merely ruminating about a distant shrub. We are the unorthodox gardeners who don't feel compulsion to pull out campion among the delphiniums; we can idle away vacantly small chunks of time without fretting about an outcrop of buttercups groping at the pulsatillas. Freedom to loll goes with random gardening, it goes with the modicum of chaos which I long to see here and there in more gardens.

. . . So when I make a plea for havoc, what would be lost? Merely the pristine appearance of a garden kept highly manicured which could be squandered for amiable disorder. Just in some places. Just to give a pull at our primeval senses. A mild desire for amorphous confusion which will gently infiltrate and, given time, one day will set the garden singing.

—from *A Gentle Plea for Chaos,* 1988

Artful Disorder

BY VITA SACKVILLE-WEST

A Chinese gardener once observed to Sir William Chambers that as our clothes are artificial, so must a garden differ likewise from the vulgar simplicity of nature. This remark gives one to ponder. To what extent does one want one's garden trim and tidy?

Opinions seem to differ. Some people are so madly wild-flower minded as to encourage such invasive things as celandine, which one must agree looks extremely pretty with its varnished golden face in the right place, on a bank under a hedgerow for instance, but not as a plant smothering more precious things in one's garden.

Then there are dead-nettles. You have to be a very high-brow gardener indeed to like dead-nettles. Personally I prefer every nettle of every kind dead and eradicated, but then I must confess to a preference for keeping my garden weedless and tidy.

It isn't that I don't like sweet disorder, but it has to be judiciously arranged. I like things to toss about freely, if such is their nature, but I do also like to see the underneath flawlessly neat and clean. I like to see young trees clear of grass at their roots, giving them a chance to receive rain. I like to see the verges of lawns sharply cut, because a lawn demands a strict formality. I don't like to see ground-elder poking up its ugly leaf among irises, its favourite domicile, knowing by some devilish instinct how hard it is going to be to dig it out. I don't like coltsfoot, with leaves as large as soup plates. I don't like bindweed, with long tapeworm roots going down deeper than one's eventual grave. And I really hate groundsel, a hideous little vulgarian for whom the only good thing to be said is that it can be so easily suppressed at birth.

There are, however, some wild plants which I encourage in my garden. The wild violets, so rightly called odorata, purple or white, I love so much that I can almost enter into the feelings of Walter Savage Landor, that man of intractable temper, who having thrown his cook out of the window exclaimed "Good God! I forgot the violets!"

Then there are the wood anemones, especially when one has the luck to find a pink sort growing in local woods. Please do not imagine me as a vandal recklessly digging up wild flowers and transplanting them with no chance of survival. I hope I know better than that, and may even claim to have saved some beauties from extermination. I would not dare to lift a Bee Orchid from its native chalk, and would pray only that no picknicker should come along and take a fancy to it.

To sum up, what have I said? That I like a tidy garden innocent of ugly or invasive weeds. That I am in favour of introducing some of our native plants so long as we know they will flourish and may be rescued from the depredation of ploughing or that even worse depredation of weed killer sprayed along our road-verges.

—from *Even More for Your Garden*, 1958

Hurrah for Vulgarity

BY CHRISTOPHER LLOYD

There are some gardeners in whose company I feel vulgar. They will expect you to fall on your knees with a magnifying glass to worship before the shrine of a spikelet of tiny green flowers with feathered margins, yet will themselves turn away disgusted from a huge, opulent quilt of hortensia hydrangeas.

I'm not against tiny flowers and I don't mind what colour they are but if they're not to be appreciated without magnification I feel they were never intended for me. I am prepared to leave them to the company of their insect pollinators.

Some people cheat. They take close-up photographs of tiny flowers and then blow them up on screen or printed page for our admiration. "How clever!" we exclaim, or are intended to exclaim. But it is the artist whom we are to admire more than the flower itself, which is seen out of context and doesn't really look like that to the naked eye at all. I have bought a close-up lens for my camera on several occasions, but I have always lost it and now conclude that I don't want to magnify the kinds of flowers I want to grow and photograph. They must have what it takes at life size and not demand an excess of peering. Even in the alps, the dazzling flowers that entrance us, though individually small, are far from modest. I have often thought that lewisias would lend themselves to bedding out, if one could get the cultural conditions right. The bed, ideally, would be vertical instead of the conventional parterre. Think how economical of space, as purchased in acres or hectares, that could be. Lewisias could occupy the south aspects, ramondas and haberleas the north, leaving us a passage just wide enough to squeeze between.

The vulgarity syndrome shows itself in colour as well as in size. A bed solid with scarlet salvias gives me no more pleasure than it probably does you, but we need bright colours in the garden all the same. Since they are so bright and draw attention to themselves so easily we don't need them in the same quantity as the cooler greys, greens and pastel shades that will set them off. The mistake in so much bedding out is to allow the scarlets, for instance, such an aggressive role. Silver foliage takes its place only as dot plants, which fidget more than they cool. The roles could be reversed, except that dot-planting is seldom a very happy arrangement.

Yellow is another colour before which people of good taste tend to quail; the bright yellow of sunflowers, gold plate achilleas and calceolarias, especially. "In general," Robin Lane Fox writes in a recent article, "the art of border-planning in well-known gardens seems to be to keep yellow to a minimum or else to isolate it in a mass during late summer." Yet what a glorious, vitalising colour it is. Why hold it at arm's length?

Writing me a postcard from the Midlands, a friend describes a visit to Chatsworth with some holidaying Germans. "In low cloud and pelting rain the Emperor fountain appeared to go up but not come down again. The double border, strictly herbaceous, in yellows with accents of orange and red, a *great* treat as we left the house. So clever; it should instantly convert doubters to yellow."

Now just imagine if those borders had concentrated on purple. They would have looked suicidally glum, beneath sodden skies.

Not when warmed by sunlight, of course, So why not, I would plead, consciously mix your colours more often? Not in a fidgety hotch-potch but in groups and treating greens and greys as colours as much as yellows, purples and the rest.

Connoisseurs of taste avoid mixtures because they are afraid of and don't know how to handle them. They might slip up. "Don't, I beg you, plant it," I remember a lady saying of a certain purple pansy, "where it can be caught in the rays of the setting sun; it sets your teeth on edge." Such dangers are multiplied by mixtures but so are the excitements and the triumphs. It's a great thing to be able to rely on your own judgement at least as much as on other people's.

Always look at the flower first. Let that speak to you on its own terms. If you like its message then think first how to grow it well, second how to fit it in with agreeable neighbours. They won't necessarily be on the same wavelength in order to get on well.

There's always a balance to be struck. I tend to think of hybrids and cultivars as man-made flowers. They inherit the weaknesses of their breeders and selectors as well as their strengths. As a wilding, a plant may have too large a preponderance of leaf and stem over flower to make much impact in a garden, which must always be acknowledged as an artificial environment. So we would like a little more flower power, and this is something that the breeder will help us to achieve.

But then, given the tools and techniques at his command and his longing for uniformity, which is one of mankind's commonest aspirations, he may go too far, reducing a plant from an individual to a unit, from an identifiable shape to an amorphous mass.

Then we must administer a sharp tug to the reins. The breeder has gone too far. We must return to nature or something near (always supposing that we haven't already accidentally destroyed it in our enthusiasm). The great thing is always to keep an open mind; never to shut ourselves deliberately away from any given class of plants, of colour, size or whatever.

If I have somewhat cut myself off from the minuscule it is doubtless because my eyesight isn't as good as forty years ago and because I have a large garden in which small things are lost. I acknowledge the place of the miniaturist but I also plead to be allowed the expansive gesture and to revel in a spot of splashing around when the mood is on me, without its being considered an unfortunate lapse by my sensitive fellow-creatures.

—from *In My Garden*, 1994

Don't Build
a Water Garden

BY REGINALD FARRER

Advice to those about to build a Water-garden—DON'T. Not that the Water-garden is not a joy and a glory; but that it is cruelly hard to keep in order and control unless you are master of millions and of broad ample acres of pool and pond. Water, like fire, is a good servant, perhaps, but is painfully liable to develop into a master. . . . How many little ponds are unguardedly built, only to become mere basins of slime and duckweed? How many larger pools are made, only to fill with *Chara, Potamogeton,* and the other noxious growths that make its depths a clogged, waving forest of dull brown verdure? The fact is a pool, not an easy thing to build and set going—is of all things in the garden the hardest of all to keep in decent order. Some of its choice inmates devour and despoil the smaller ones; water weeds increase and multiply at a prodigious rate; dead leaves drift thick upon it in autumn, slime and green horrors make a film across it in summer.

—from *Alpines and Bog Plants,* 1908

Italian Garden Magic

BY EDITH WHARTON

Though it is an exaggeration to say that there are no flowers in Italian gardens, yet to enjoy and appreciate the Italian garden-craft one must always bear in mind that it is independent of flori-culture.

The Italian garden does not exist for flowers; its flowers exist for it: they are a late and infrequent adjunct to its beauties, a parenthetical grace counting only as one more touch in the general effect of enchantment. This is no doubt partly explained by the difficulty of cultivating any but spring flowers in so hot and dry a climate, and the result has been a wonderful development of the more permanent effects to be obtained from the three other factors in garden-composition—marble, water and perennial verdure— and the achievement, by their skillful blending, of a charm inde-pendent of the seasons.

It is hard to explain to the modern garden-lover, whose whole conception of the charm of gardens is formed of successive pictures of flower-loveliness, how this effect of enchantment can be produced by anything so dull and monotonous as a mere combination of clipped green and stone work.

The traveler returning from Italy, with his eyes and imagination full of the ineffable Italian garden-magic, knows vaguely that the enchantment exists; that he has been under its spell, and that it is more potent, more enduring, more intoxicating to every sense than the most elaborate and glowing effects of modern horticulture; but he may not have found the key to the mystery. Is it because the sky is bluer, because the vegetation is more luxuriant? Our midsummer skies are almost as deep, our foliage is as rich, and perhaps more varied; there are, indeed, not a few resemblances between the North American summer climate and that of Italy in spring and autumn.

Some of those who have fallen under the spell are inclined to ascribe the Italian garden-magic to the effect of time; but, wonder-working as this undoubtedly is, it leaves many beauties unaccounted for. To seek the answer one must go deeper: the garden must be studied in relation to the house, and both in relation to the landscape. The garden of the Middle Ages, the garden one sees in old missal illuminations and in early woodcuts, was a mere patch of ground within the castle precincts, where "simples" were grown around a central well-head and fruit was espaliered against the walls. But in the rapid flowering of Italian civilization the castle walls were soon thrown down, and the garden expanded, taking in the fish pond, the bowling green, the rose arbor and the clipped walk. The Italian country house, especially in the center and the south of Italy, was almost always built on a hillside, and one day the architect looked forth from the terrace of his villa, and saw that, in his survey of the garden, the enclosing landscape was naturally included: the two formed a part of the same composition.

The recognition of this fact was the first step in the development of the great garden art of the Renaissance: the next was the architect's discovery of the means by which nature and art might be fused in his picture. He had now three problems to deal with: his garden must be adapted to the architectural lines of the house it adjoined; it must be adapted to the requirements of the inmates of the house, in the sense of providing shady walks, sunny bowling greens, parterres and orchards, all conveniently accessible; and lastly it must be adapted to the landscape around it. At no time and in no country has this triple problem been so successfully dealt with as in the treatment of the Italian country house from the beginning of the sixteenth to the end of the eighteenth century; and in the blending of different elements, the subtle transition from the fixed and formal lines of art to the shifting and irregular lines of nature, and lastly in the essential convenience and livableness of the garden, lies the fundamental secret of the old garden-magic.

However much other factors may contribute to the total impression of charm, yet by eliminating them one after another, by *thinking away* the flowers, the sunlight, the rich tinting of time, one finds that, underlying all these, there is a deeper harmony of design which is independent of any adventitious effects. This does not imply that a plan of an Italian garden is as beautiful as the garden itself. The more permanent materials of which the latter is made— the stonework, the evergreen foliage, the effects of rushing or motionless water, above all the lines of the natural scenery—all form a part of the artist's design. But these things are as beautiful at one season as at another; and even these are but the accessories of the fundamental plan. The inherent beauty of the garden lies in the grouping of its parts—in the converging lines of its long ilex walks, the alternation of sunny open spaces with cool woodland shade, the proportion between terrace and bowling green, or between the height of a wall and the width of a path. None of these details was negligible to the landscape architect of the Renaissance: he considered the distribution of shade and sunlight, of straight lines of masonry and rippled lines of foliage, as carefully as he weighed the relation of his whole composition to the scene about it.

Then, again, any one who studies the old Italian gardens will be struck with the way in which the architect broadened and simplified his plan if it faced a grandiose landscape. Intricacy of detail, complicated groupings of terraces, fountains, labyrinths and porticoes, are found in sites where there is no great sweep of landscape attuning the eye to larger impressions. The farther north one goes, the less grand the landscape becomes and the more elaborate the garden. The great pleasure-grounds overlooking the Roman Campagna are laid out on severe and majestic lines: the parts are few; the total effect is one of breadth and simplicity.

It is because, in the modern revival of gardening, so little attention has been paid to these first principles of the art that the garden lover should not content himself with a vague enjoyment of old Italian gardens, but should try to extract from them principles which may be applied at home. He should observe, for instance, that the old Italian garden was meant to be lived in—a use to which, at least in America, the modern garden is seldom put. He should note that, to this end, the grounds were as carefully and conveniently planned as the house, with broad paths (in which two or more could go abreast) leading from one division to another; with shade easily accessible from the house, as well as a sunny sheltered walk for winter; and with effective transitions from the dusk of wooded alleys to open flowery spaces or to the level sward of the bowling green. He should remember that the terraces and formal gardens adjoined the house, that the ilex or laurel walks beyond were clipped into shape to effect a transition between the straight lines of masonry and the untrimmed growth of the woodland to which they led, and that each step away from architecture was a nearer approach to nature.

The cult of the Italian garden has spread from England to America, and there is a general feeling that, by placing a marble bench here and a sun-dial there, Italian "effects" may be achieved. The results produced, even where much money and thought have been expended, are not altogether satisfactory; and some critics have thence inferred that the Italian garden is, so to speak, *untranslatable*, that it cannot be adequately rendered in another landscape and another age.

Certain effects, those which depend on architectural grandeur as well as those due to coloring and age, are no doubt unattainable; but there is, nonetheless, much to be learned from the old Italian gardens, and the first lesson is that, if they are to be a real inspiration, they must be copied, not in the letter but in the spirit. That is, a marble sarcophagus and a dozen twisted columns will not make an Italian garden; but a piece of ground laid out and planted on the principles of the old garden-craft will be, not indeed an Italian garden in the literal sense, but, what is far better, *a garden as well adapted to its surroundings as were the models which inspired it.*

This is the secret to be learned from the villas of Italy; and no one who has looked at them with this object in view will be content to relapse into vague admiration of their loveliness. As Browning, in passing Cape St. Vincent and Trafalgar Bay, cried out:

> Here and here did England help me: how can I help
> England?—say,

so the garden lover, who longs to transfer something of the old garden-magic to his own patch of ground at home, will ask himself, in wandering under the umbrella pines of the Villa Borghese, or through the box parterres of the Villa Lante: What can I bring away from here? And the more he studies and compares, the more inevitably will the answer be: "Not this or that amputated statue, or broken *bas relief,* or fragmentary effect of any sort, but a sense of the informing spirit—an understanding of the gardener's purpose, and of the uses to which he meant his garden to be put.

—from *Italian Villas and Their Gardens,* 1904

SEASONS IN THE GARDEN

New feet within my garden go
New fingers stir the sod;
A troubadour upon the elm
Betrays the solitude.

New children play upon the green,
New weary sleep below;
And still the pensive spring returns,
And still the punctual snow!

—EMILY DICKINSON c.1881

February

BY JOSEPH WOOD KRUTCH

The most serious charge which can be brought against New England is not Puritanism but February. It is true that before we are finished with it the days are unmistakably longer than they were in December or January, and true that there are periods when the daylight is brighter, as well as longer. But these brief interludes are too infrequent to be counted on, and the relapses are so complete that the interludes do not seem even promises. Now more than ever one must remind oneself that it is wasteful folly to wish that time would pass, or—as the puritanical old saying used to have it—to kill time until time kills you. Spring is too far away to comfort even by anticipation, and winter long ago lost the charm of novelty. This is the very three A.M. of the calendar.

I will not say that I would like to dispense with February, for I should not willingly agree to make my life one-twelfth shorter—not even, I suppose, if it were going to be February all the year round. Nevertheless there are regions of the earth where the months bear the same names as ours but where the allotment

141

of time to the various seasons has been more sensibly managed. Some of them, for instance, have a real November (in December), and a real December (in January), and then get on immediately to an April. That seems to me about right, and I would gladly exchange our February for another May; or, if that is asking too much, for another October; or for, indeed, almost anything else I was offered. There are some optimists who search eagerly for the skunk cabbage which in February sometimes pushes itself up through the ice, and who call it a sign of spring. I wish that I could feel that way about it, but I do not. The truth of the matter, to me, is simply that skunk cabbage blooms in the winter time. There is no more cold-blooded animal than your frog, and you will not catch him stirring now.

—from *The Twelve Seasons*, 1949

The Onset of Spring

BY ELIZABETH LAWRENCE

In the South we go in quest of spring as soon as Christmas is past and the new year begins. The first days of January find us searching among the last fallen leaves for purple violets and white hyacinths and the yellow buds of winter aconite. And when we have found these frosty flowers close to the cold ground, we break off and carry into the house a few branches of Japanese quince with buds already swollen and ready to burst. By the time the quince buds have opened into flowers as pale as apple blossoms, their fellows in the garden may be in bloom too, if the days are warm.

Those who garden north of us wait longer for the end of winter and the delight of spring; but spring, when it comes, follows much the same pattern, and all eager gardeners will be in quest of it. Those who stay indoors until the golden flames of forsythias announce to all that spring is here will miss the first crocus (perhaps the silver and lavender of *Crocus sieberi,* perhaps the brown and gold of *C. susianus,* the early blue of squills and chionodoxas, and the pleasure of being surprised by the snowdrops. No matter how closely you watch for the snowdrops, you never quite catch them on the way. One day the ground is bare, and the next time you look, the nodding buds are ready to open!

A tiny hyacinth that looks like a grape hyacinth blooms with the first little bulbs of the season. This is *Hyacinthus ciliatus* whose clear blue spikes repeat the blue of *Nemophila*—if I sow this lovely annual in the fall so that the first blossoms come early. At the same time (late February), there is a creamy white violet in bloom in Southern gardens. No one seems to know its name or provenience, but I advise all those interested in violets to search it out and make up to its possessors, for I know of no other sort so white or so early or so beautiful.

Late in February or early in March, the brilliant purple of *Iris reticulata* appears in the rock garden. It needs yellow for contrast, and I plant it with campernelles and the best and earliest of the alyssums, *A. wulfenianum,* or with yellow pansies. To bloom early and close to the ground with the little bulbs, there are other precious rock plants. For blue there is blue-eyed Mary (*Omphalodes verna*); for pink, of course, the various tints of moss pink (*Phlox subulata*); and for white, *Arabis alpina,* which sometimes begins to flower with me as early as the end of January, but usually comes into bloom a month later.

Here the first daffodil to bloom is the short-stemmed pale yellow trumpet that grows in most old gardens. It comes with the crocuses and early shrubs, and has been in bloom the last days of January. But that was a season when the onset of spring ended before it seemed possible. As a rule, this little early trumpet is at its best in February, and is quickly followed by other early sorts. . . . With us, daffodils are in bloom by the middle of March. They bloom before the leaves are on the trees, and the shrubs that bloom with them are leafless too.

Very early in the spring, the purple-leaf plum is in flower with the saucer magnolia, Japanese quince, forsythia, and Thunberg's spirea. By this time, the common primrose is in bloom (late February or early March with us; late April in the vicinity of Boston) with perennial candytuft and black-purple pansies. Dutch hyacinths bloom with daffodils. I often wonder why they are not more generally planted. The soft tints are charming in combination with early spring flowers, and they are a welcome change from so much yellow. Late in March, the silvery blue of the hyacinth 'Electra' is delightful with pale yellow primroses of the Munstead strain and white candytuft.

When the daffodils are waning and the tulips coloring, dogwood and pearl bush, flowering almond, snowflakes, and the early white iris are at their best, and trees and trellises are dripping with purple wisteria. Then spring is in full flower with tulips, lilacs, and flowering crab-apples, followed closely by peony, iris, and mock orange.

—from *The Home Garden,* February 1943

The Month of May

BY RICHARDSON WRIGHT

As the smell of hot leather to the huntsman, as the reek of a husband's old pipes to a widow, so is the incense of newly-turned soil to a gardener in Spring. After a Winter of city reeks and the dismal stench of muddy roads in the gum-boot days of March and early April, go forth into your vegetable garden as a devotee into a church. Discard all the clothes the temperature and your proximity to neighbors will allow. Have the feet well booted. Drive the fork straight down till its tines disappear. Lift the clod. Clout it. And around you arises the incense of the soil, which is better than all the perfumes of the East.

Were I a millionaire, and could I afford a host of gardeners, I would never permit them to perform this initial rite for me. For strange as it may seem, this benison of the nostrils can come only in its fullest beauty to those who turn the soil themselves. Merely walking across a newly-plowed meadow or a newly-spaded garden patch brings only a weak suggestion of that earth perfume. Its enjoyment is inextricably commingled with the rhythm of the body's

146

swinging, the play of muscles, the lash of the sun on the arms and back and neck, the clutch of the fingers, the delight of the eye as the brown earth is turned to the sun, the delight of the skin in its gross sweat.

—from *The Gardener's Bed-Book*, 1929

Rain After Drought

BY GERTRUDE JEKYLL

"Thou sentest a gracious rain upon thine inheritance; and refreshedst it when it was weary."

The whole garden is singing this hymn of praise and thankfulness. It is the middle of June; no rain had fallen for nearly a month, and our dry soil had become a hot dust above, a hard cake below. A burning wind from the east that had prevailed for some time, had brought quantities of noisome blight, and had left all vegetation, already parched with drought, a helpless prey to the devouring pest. Bushes of garden Roses had their buds swarming with green-fly, and all green things, their leaves first coated and their pores clogged with viscous stickiness, and then covered with adhering wind-blown dust, were in a pitiable state of dirt and suffocation. But last evening there was a gathering of grey cloud, and this ground of grey was traversed by those fast-travelling wisps of fleecy blackness that are the surest promise of near rain the sky can show. By bedtime rain was falling steadily, and in the night it came down on the roof in a small thunder of steady downpour. It was pleasant to wake from time to time and hear the welcome sound, and to know that the clogged leaves were being washed clean, and that their pores were once more drawing in the breath of life, and that the thirsty roots were drinking their fill. And now, in the morning, how good it is to see the brilliant light of the blessed summer day, always brightest just after rain, and to see how every tree and plant is full of new life and abounding gladness; and to feel one's own thankfulness of heart, and that it is good to live, and all the more good to live in a garden.

What is one to say about June—the time of perfect young summer, the fulfillment of the promise of the earlier months, and with as yet no sign to remind one that its fresh young beauty will ever fade? For my own part I wander up into the wood and say, "June is here—June is here; thank God for lovely June!" The soft cooing of the wood-dove, the glad song of many birds, the flitting of butterflies, the hum of all the little winged people among the branches, the sweet earth-scents—all seem to say the same, with an endless reiteration, never wearying because so gladsome. It is the offering of the Hymn of Praise! The lizards run in and out of the heathy tufts in the hot sunshine, and as the long day darkens the night-jar trolls out his strange song, so welcome because it is the prelude to the perfect summer night; here and there a glow-worm shows its little lamp. June is here—June is here; thank God for lovely June!

—from *Home and Garden*, 1900

Summer

BY ROBERT DASH

June gardens are so bright and shining and clear that they seem incapable of aging. Their physicality is everywhere beguiling and as much as they are demanding, as much as the gardener must be swift with all of his work, there is so much joy in it, the stripling growth so responsive to the smallest of ministrations that his fatigue seems to get submerged by elation and is at most a fugitive thing. It is satisfying to bend and tie the first long cane of the roses, plot and space a little park of sticky cleome, try new plantings in new beds, see last year's seed-grown clematis take off and throw bloom after bloom. But the slowing is equally rapid. By mid-July and all through August, a gardener's chores are without innovation and become large in repetition, the same thing done at the same spot, over and over. Maturity is in the green frame of the garden and work is entirely custodial in nature, rather like housekeeping, a matter of spit and polish and the higher your standards, the more minute the work. If there are enough pale or white flowers the full evening hours may become the only truly pleasing ones. It is cooler then. Dead-heading, pinching, pulling crabgrass from paths and lawn, watering, watering, watering, sweeping terraces are chores done in stillness and heat. One feels like a moldy figurine in a terrarium. One thinks of letting it all go and waiting for September.

But so many unexpected little felicities remain as one passes from bush to bush, composition to composition, through units of ingratiation one had planned so carefully through the long winter months. It is certainly a time for the hammock but it seems to stay permanently soaked from the sprinkler. Three perfect, perfectly ripe tomatoes come in on a morning but then fifteen by the end of the week, twenty the next and then the birds mercifully begin taking pokes out of them and one stops trying to fob them off on one's friends. Potato bugs will take care of the rest, later.

One waits for the sound of thunder and sudden ill winds and begins to track Caribbean storms as they hover and dart up the Eastern Seaboard. Birches seem singed more than in other years and their leaves and willow leaves are down everywhere and then the single ginkgo one moved last autumn suddenly breaks from its deadwood the last week in July to resurrect one's feelings. An enormous thistle tree shows purple and is flecked with pairs of finches streaming through the stems searching for nesting down. When they find none as yet, they loop to Queen Anne's lace as if white anything might do. One thinks of dense, satisfying, deep and cool salads but the lettuce has once again bolted and sprouts from later plantings are still too small. The arugula is doing well but heat has deepened the flavor and made it sharp. One makes alarming mixtures of chard, fennel tops, parsley, central young leaves of endive, feathers of burnet and great chunks of white, entirely sweet onions. Young garlic are sliced in lengths from root to stem through the blades like scallions. And some bell peppers, no matter how small.

Days are dry, dusty, but mornings soak in fog and dew.

Mornings have odors, noons do not. The *Magnolia grandiflora* has two more buds left, and three *Magnolia liliiflora* are out for the second time but their flowers blister and scald in the sun. By eight the sky is pale metal and a curious wobbling and rippling seems invested in the horizon like a roll of more heat. More dust settles on the leaves of bergamot but this darkening makes the blooms seem brighter. Catbirds have taken the last of the currants from the new hedge near the new terrace and one thinks of changing the pattern of the tiles on the old, which now is hardly ever used. Or, of covering the stones in a sheet of water a few inches deep as if a clear spring had welled there. The umbels of elephant garlic are higher by a foot and, beaten down by wind or not, quiver with bees.

Mid-July through August the garden seems to be a thick, stodgy parade, with all of its outlines dulled and clouded. It seems to lumber along muffled in too much rich living and all of its greens begin to mature and shade like drifts of snow in January twilight. I don't know quite why, but optimum foliage has always rather bored me, perhaps because ends for me have never been as important as the means one needs to acquire them. It is like the long, fat summer book whose passages one hoped would go on forever but one whose theme gets to seem a drowned or buried thing. A simplicity seems lost and covered. In the streets and highways of summer the world is similarly costumed. Neither birds nor cars nor machines nor people are still. A pageantry, if you will, sometimes lovely, sometimes not. It will be over soon. Pods of seeds are forming. I have seen sweaters.

—from *The East Hampton Star*, July 29, 1985

July

BY JOE ECK AND
WAYNE WINTERROWD

The temperament that makes up all serious gardeners must have a large component of melancholy. For however glorious the garden's display might be, the true gardener seems always to look behind with regret at what has passed and ahead with longing at what is to come. To be squarely anchored in the moment, to savor just what lies before one and want nothing more—this must be a great bliss for those who possess the ability. Certainly it is true, even for the most brooding of gardeners, that the conjunction of a perfect day, a good stint at weeding, and perhaps some unlooked-for success with a difficult plant can make one feel, for a little time, that the garden is, just as it is, enough. Alas, though it may be otherwise for many gardeners, for us such moments are fleeting, and no more at our command than a perfect night's rest, the return of love, or that lift of the heart one experiences at the brief recapture— through a fragrance, a bar of music, an old book with one's name in it—of the sensations of youth.

Generally we move through our garden at the height of our splendid but brief summer with a strong sense that it is all so transitory, that it goes by so fast, leaving us with hardly a chance to catch our breath before it is gone. By a leap of faith not too hard to bring off, we trust that the garden will be here next year, even richer with beauty, even fuller of pleasure. A slightly harder leap assures us, somewhat, that we will be here too, to make it happen and to glory in our success. The hardest leap of all is to believe that the garden might endure after us, for a time at least, giving pleasure to someone else, who might work on its canvas a whole new range of beauty we have not even dreamed of. For most of that we will simply have to wait to see.

. . . July is one of the great hinges of the gardening year— perhaps the greatest. There are others, for in gardening the relationship between past and future comes into focus more clearly than it seems to in other pursuits of life. The two other periods that most clearly mark transitions for the gardener are April and September. They tend to be mostly unmixed in character: April brings the awareness that all that one wishes to achieve still lies ahead, while September brings a sort of tranquillity, a sense that the garden—still lovely, certainly—has been as much as one had a right to expect, and maybe more. But between April's youthful optimism and September's mature acceptance comes July; characterized both by longing and by hope, it constitutes a sort of horticultural midlife crisis.

Shame on us, perhaps, for being so confused by the beauty of July. For the weather then is lovely, perhaps the loveliest of the year for those who crave warmth. There is a predictability to the brightness of the sun that one experiences in no other season, one faultless day breaking after another. There is real heat, the kind that puts an end to garden chores (for us, at least, who are not used to it) and offers a quiet, restorative day at the river. Rain still falls, but it occurs late in the day or when we are sleeping, the earth's risen moisture returning to it as thunderstorms crashing against the mountains. Best of all, we wake some mornings to find that a cloud has settled into the garden, trapped against our hillside until the sun's rays dissipate it in milky streams, leaving the garden wet with its moisture and every spider web silvered over.

The garden, too, is richer with flowers than it has been before or will be again. Much of the perfection of June remains with us, for cool nights cause the blooms of roses, geraniums, verbascums, and dianthus to linger. The flowers of high summer, the platycodons, monardas, border phlox, and thistly eryngiums, will just be showing color, and Joe Pye weed will be purpling the roadsides and the garden by the end of the month. Even those flowers planted for their autumn bloom will count for something, not as bloom but as a promise. The native asters have just branched into flowering stems, and *Aster lateriflorus* 'Horizontalis' has assumed the substantiality, almost, of boxwood. *Sedum telephium purpureum* 'Autumn Joy', planted in every garden but still indispensable, will have attained its full height, its waxy celadon leaves surmounted by pale florets like broccoli past its prime. Much lies before and, really, not too much behind.

But still we note, and sadly, that the sunrise, though usually glorious, comes a little later each morning. By the adjustment of an internal clock we always find curious, we tend to sleep a little later in the morning, rising not at half past four or five, but at six, or seven. As the month advances, darkness may catch us still at dinner, and the magical twilight rambles of June are replaced by moonlit walks instead. We begin to read again, not garden books and certainly not catalogs, though those offering bulbs have begun to arrive and are carefully put aside. There's a little more music on the stereo in the evening. We go to bed a little earlier.

—from *A Year at North Hill*, 1995

The Arrival of Fall

BY LAUREN SPRINGER

Fresh, vibrant June passes to a languid, slow July. Then comes a turning point, when summer suddenly feels utterly tiresome. Some years, late summer weather is kind and merciful, indulging the gardener in a quick turn to cool nights and days filled with a mellow, amber sunlight that actually feels good on the face, totally unlike the prickling and piercing rays of high summer. Other years, the wait is interminable, summer's heat oozing on well into months traditionally autumnal.

     Autumn has become my favorite time of the year. It took a while for negative associations with the beginning of the school year to wane, for the golden sunlight and foliage to stop conjuring up the intestinal butterflies that went along with similarly toned school buses lurching down the street. While some find spring with all its optimistic beginnings the finest season in the garden, I much prefer the unfrenzied pace of fall. In the spring, it is easy to feel overwhelmed by the sudden demands of the garden. A long winter has a way of creating such great yearnings and high expectations that I could almost say I feel a bit pressured by the new season, not to mention out of shape after a lazy winter spent fattening up by the fire. By autumn, I'm synchronized with the garden, lean and mean, realistic about my expectations. The garden requires much less of me — weeds are well under control and careful deadheading has long been abandoned. As a friend once described so well, the autumn garden is a machete garden. Anyone still trying to control or tame it in September is either hopelessly deluded or has a strange need to use large cutting tools from the jungle. The season transforms the garden and the gardener. While a similar scene in June might send one scrambling for stakes and twine, come September it is a wonderful sense of release to watch plants collapse slowly on each other, soft and heavy with the weight of a full season's growth. Leaves begin to yellow and brown. Flowers become seeds. Everything is soft, large, ripe. As I walk among the plants, they reflect my mood — placid and self-satisfied.

Fall isn't all retrospective mellowness. It is also a time for renewed activity. As the oppressive heat wanes, rediscovered energy can be put to great use, and not just for the traditional autumnal rite of bulb planting. Seed collecting kicks into high gear. Autumn is also the best time to assess the garden and decide which plants need to be moved, divided or tossed out altogether. Plants are at their largest, and crowding is painfully evident. A plant from which one waited patiently for some sign of beauty can now be given the old heave-ho without reservations if it has failed to perform. Integrating new plants is easier than ever; a full, live picture lies before the gardener, helping inspire good combinations as compared to the spring, when tiny, barely awakened leaf rosettes require calling upon strong imaging powers to visualize what may develop later. Most plants relish the chance to put out good roots without the competition of top growth and moisture-sapping heat. The soil stays warm much longer than the air, giving fall-planted individuals a long season of underground growth and establishment. If it weren't for the fact that some plants are not available in the fall, I would probably stop almost all my spring planting. Even small transplanted seedlings, given the benefit of some mulch around their base, have done remarkably well when planted in the fall.

Autumn is a time when warm color and rustling sounds resonate throughout the plant world. In the deciduous woodlands of the East and Midwest, winter spreads down the land from north to south, from highland to lowland, rolling a carpet of foliage color over the landscape before it. The land, so serenely green for all those months, suddenly looks like an infrared photograph. On the grasslands of the prairie and plains, the tired gray-green and buff of late summer take on richer amber, sienna and rust tones as the foliage and seedheads of the grasses ripen. Late-blooming wild-flowers, predominantly deep golds and purples, attract sleepy butterflies and bees, while more energetic birds frenetically gorge themselves on seeds before the first snow cover blankets the land.

The sun arcs lower in the sky, softening and burnishing the light. All colors seem to emanate an inner warmth as if the heat of the summer were stored within them. The most mundane scenes —an empty concrete basketball court alive with whirling, wind-blown leaves, a chocolate-brown field spiked with tawny corn stubble—take on the qualities of gold leaf, the light of a Venetian Renaissance painting.

The lower sun also creates lovely lighting effects in the garden. While in summer it would be suppertime before any similar effect might be possible, now mid- and late afternoon becomes a time for backlit drama. Grass panicles glisten and shimmer when touched by the slanted light; foliage reds and golds are intensified as the sun passes through them; fragile petals resemble halos given this autumnal spotlight.

Just as fall is a time for letting go, for riding with the slow, melancholy yet beautiful decline toward the inevitability of winter, it is also a time for loosening up rigid color rules. What may jar in the May and June garden is a welcome sight in October. Colors have richened and deepened with the cooler temperatures and golden light. The sunlight of autumn softens the boundaries that in spring and summer define orange, red, magenta and purple. The gardener should soften as well. Just as a person living out his or her last years should be indulged some special extravagances and not judged harshly for them, so should an autumnal garden be allowed a grand finale of wild color fireworks without too many "tasteful" restraints. Nature combines cobalt skies, red and yellow leaves and purple asters; the gardener does well to take inspiration from these stunning scenes.

Form and texture take on their most important roles this time of the year—seedheads, flower stalks and the mature size of the plants create a sense of fullness, of tactile and visual abundance. Grasses hiss and rattle in the breezes like so many whispering crones. I chuckle thinking of the overexcited Halloweeners soon to pass by the ravenna grass and miscanthus clumps. Not only are the grasses large enough to hide a menacing creature, their wind-borne voices are sure to strike fear in the more imaginative and suggestible trick-or-treaters. The sweet civility of Christmas, with its parade of guests to kiss and horrible velvet jumpers to wear, scored a distant second on my childhood holiday rankings, far behind the front-runner, Halloween. Those seemingly interminable dark walks between houses, long before street-lit safety became an issue, were more adrenalizing than the mountains of candy filling the sack. Sadly Halloween, with our good-natured attempts to protect the little ones from the increasingly dangerous traffic and increasingly sick adults, has become an utter bore. Children show up listlessly at the door with parents in tow. Well-lit malls and gymnasiums filled with high-tech scary props that now often host the event will never equal those unchaperoned nights spent running from whispering, chattering, cackling plant life.

Back in the garden, a frosty morning transforms all things hairy, spiny, silver. Prickly pear, snowball and claret-cup cactus are caught in a crystalline net of hoary spines. Lambs ears, santolina and *Salvia argentea* glisten in the weak early sunlight. The artemisias, a frosty sight even in the heat of summer, take on an ethereal quality. *Artemisia caucasica*, a four-inch shrublet, and huge four-foot *A.* × 'Powis Castle' are the laciest. Whitest are ground-hugging *A. stellerana* and 18-inch *A.* × 'Valerie Finnis'. Prettiest of all, though, is the sparkling silver skeleton of 'Silver King' artemisia's flower panicles. The foliage of this plant is nice, but I can find silver in many other plants less inclined to bossiness in the garden. The only reason I tolerate this spreading garden thug (and only in one small, isolated spot) is for those delicate flower stalks that appear late in the summer and remain until the first heavy snow flattens them. Their airy effect is intensified on those mornings when hoarfrost transforms the landscape and they look like white plumes of chilled breath from the garden.

Two very distinct autumn scenes dominate my garden. The east-facing rose garden offers lingering pastel perennials and frost-tolerant annuals among the last cabbagy heads of various peach, pink, yellow and white ever-blooming David Austin roses. On the other side of the house, in the warm western sun, grasses, late-blooming perennials and tough annuals in hot colors—indigo-blue, red, orange, gold, purple—burn brightly until well into November when a pummeling of successive hard frosts and snowy dustings finally extinguish them. The two areas couldn't be any more different in mood.

—from *The Undaunted Garden*, 1994

October

BY CAROL BISHOP HIPPS

Bittersweet October. The mellow, messy, leaf-kicking, perfect pause between the opposing miseries of summer and winter. Mornings (some of them) start off foggy, the cold, soaked bumblebees buried, immobile, in the flower faces or maybe bumbling around in the mulch, dirty and barely able to crawl, like drowsy drunks. Along the creek hordes of just-back-from-somewhere starlings converse squeakily and incessantly as they breakfast among the hackberries.

The wind comes up with the sun, batting away the fog and driving the ash leaves down, shower after golden shower, onto the lawn and into the street, where they hiss along the pavement.

In the bed surrounding the Japanese maple the reinvigorated sweet alyssum and ageratum foam like waves breaking around a warm-toned island of golden marigold, lantana, and melampodium, piping-hot orange emilia, waxen red dahlia, and antique white, orange-centered 'Star White' zinnia.

The Japanese anemone 'Honorine Jobert', which looked so

frail and hopeless when I planted her in March, has a few holes in her leaves, but she proudly waves a half-dozen pearllike flower buds and at least as many ivory-skinned blossoms. Shows how much *I* know.

Roses revive, blooming as if they're convinced May has come again.

A wild, anarchistic beauty seizes the neighborhood. The dry leaves blow where they will, even onto the neatest lawns; an army of leaf-blowing landscape technicians couldn't deter them. The crape myrtles (surely they must be tired from all that blooming), turn russet-orange, and, Cinderella at the ball, the common mulberry, so drab and unappreciated the remainder of the year, suddenly (briefly) glows brilliant yellow, a beacon of splendor.

In the late afternoon sun the mountain above us is a rusty amalgam of old-gold hickory, ruby-red dogwood, firelit sugar maple, pink and orange persimmon, and the fruit basket hues of sassafras. The smoketrees along the winding roadsides are all fire and no smoke now, while, nearer ground level, *Salvia azurea*, as intensely blue as the October sky, mixes with the reblooming butterfly weed and prairie coneflower.

In the fields Queen Anne's lace blooms anew with the golden aster. The velvet-stemmed staghorn sumac discards its red and purple leaves but holds the cones of furry, blood-red fruit, to be meted out to the birds once winter settles in.

—from *In a Southern Garden,* 1994

A Fire by Ice

BY JAMAICA KINCAID

It is winter in Vermont, and so my garden does not exist. In its place are mounds of white, the raised beds covered with snow, as in a graveyard—not a graveyard in New England, with its orderliness and neatness and sense of that's that, but a graveyard in the place I am from, a warm place. There, a grave is topped off with a huge mound of loose earth—carelessly, as if piled up in child's play, not serious at all—because death is just another way of being, and the dead will not stay put, and sometimes the actions of the dead are more significant, more profound, than their actions in life, and no structure of concrete or stone can contain them.

The whiteness of the snow is an eraser, so that I am in a state of near-disbelief. A clump of lovage, with its tall, thick stalks of celerylike leaves (with celerylike taste), did really stand next to the hedge of rhubarb; the potatoes were near the rhubarb, the broccoli was near the potatoes, the carrots and beets were together and near the potatoes, the basil and cilantro were together and near the peas; the tomatoes were in a bed by themselves (a long, narrow strip that I made all by myself this summer with a new little tiller I bought from Gardener's Supply Company), separating my garden from my daughter Annie's; the strawberries were in a bed by themselves, and so were all the salad greens; the sunflowers, tall and short, in various hues of yellow and brown, were clustered in groups over here, over there, and over here again. The scarecrow that scared nothing was here; the gun to shoot the things the scarecrow didn't scare was right here (unloaded, lying between the bundles of hay for mulching the potatoes). The line of silver (aluminum pie plates) was strung between the two tepees covered with lima-bean vines (whose pods remained empty of beans).

The colors (the green of leaf, the red-pink stem of rhubarb, the red veins of beet leaves, the yellows and browns of sunflowers) start out tentatively, in a maybe-or-maybe-not way, and then one day, perhaps after a heavy rain, everything is strong and itself, twinkling, jewel-like. At that moment, I think life will never change: it will always be summer. The families of rabbits or woodchucks will eat the salad greens just before they are ready to be picked; I plot ways to kill these animals but can never bring myself to do it; I decide to build a fence around the garden and then decide not to. There are more or fewer Japanese beetles than last year—who can really care? There are too many zucchini—who can really care? And then, as if it had never happened before, I hear that the temperature will drop to such a low degree that it will cause a frost.

I always take this personally; I think a frost is something someone is doing to me—only to me. And this is how winter in the garden begins—with another tentativeness, a curtsy to the actual cold to come, a gentle form of it. The effect of the cold air on things growing in the garden is something I cannot get used to, cannot understand, even after so many years. How can it be that after a frost the entire garden looks as if it had been to a party in Hell? As if it had been picked up and set down just outside the furnace of a baker's oven, with the fire constantly fed and the oven door never shut?

I must have been about ten years old when I first came in contact with cold air. Where I lived (Antigua), the air was hot and then hotter, and if sometimes—usually in December—the temperature at night got down to seventy-five degrees you wore a sweater, and a flannel blanket was put on the bed. Once, the parents of a girl I knew got a refrigerator, and when they were not at home she asked me to come and put my hand in the freezer part. I was convinced then (and remain so now) that cold air is unnatural, man-made, associated with prosperity (refrigerators being common in the prosperous North), and more real (as the artificial always seems) and special than the warm air that was so ordinary to me. And then (when I moved to the prosperous North) I became suspicious of cold air, because it seemed also associated with the dark. With the cold comes the dark. In the dark, things grow pale and die, and no explanation, from science or nature, of how the sun can shine brightly in the deep of winter has ever been satisfactory to me. In my heart I know that the cold and the light, the winter and the summer, cannot be at the same time.

—from *The New Yorker*, February 22, 1993

THE BOUNTY OF THE GARDEN

The June nights are long and warm; the roses flowering; and the gardens full of lust and bees, mingling in the asparagus beds.

—*VIRGINIA WOOLF*, DIARIES

Earth laughs in flowers.

—*RALPH WALDO EMERSON*, 1847

A Garden Song
(to W.E.H.)

BY AUSTIN DOBSON

Here, in this sequestered close,
Bloom the hyacinth and rose;
Here beside the modest stock
Flaunts the flaring hollyhock;
Here, without a pang, one sees
Ranks, conditions, and degrees.

All the seasons run their race
In this quiet resting-place;
Peach, and apricot, and fig
Here will ripen, and grow big;
Here is store and overplus—
More had not Alcinous!

Here, in alleys cool and green,
Far ahead the thrush is seen;
Here along the southern wall
Keeps the bee his festival;
All is quiet else—afar
Sounds of toil and turmoil are.

Here be shadows large and long;
Here be spaces meet for song;
Grant, O garden-god, that I,
Now that none profane is nigh—
Now that mood and moment please,
Find the fair Pierides!

—1895

Childhood Roses

BY M.F.K. FISHER

The first rose I remember that my mother loved was what she called, in her inimitable Anglo-Dresden accent, a Frau Karl Druschki. Then I remember the Cecile Brunners, or, as she pronounced the name, Sessle Br-r-rooners, rolling the *r* in her slightly operatic German. They were lovely, tight, little curly things like pink shells, multi-petaled, of course. They grew on pergolas and trellises everywhere, and used to snag tall people's hair. They were wonderful on May Day for the baskets we hung on old ladies' doors.

When we first went to Whittier, in about 1911, the county roads were still bordered with the free roses that senators and mayors and chambers of commerce begged the few orange ranchers and farmers to plant. They said, "Plant, plant, *plant!* People will come out from Iowa and think this is an earthly paradise!" And the free donations grew almost frantically, and then died of neglect. By 1918, when we moved down Painter Avenue to the Ranch, there were still roses along the roads. It never occurred to any of the ranchers to spray, irrigate, clip, prune. They *grew* the tag end of them, so beautiful: the Frau Karl Druschki; the common, bright scarlet, lushly blooming Ragged-Robins. But best of all, in my first years, were the ones that grew over the abandoned outhouses in Whittier.

Whittier was built about a hundred years ago by a band of Quakers who proved their social standing, in one way or another at least, by whether they had one-holers or two- or three-holers in their backyard. When the flush toilet came along, somewhat before we arrived in 1911, instead of removing the latrines and covering up the good supply of night soil, the settlers simply pushed their outhouses over, filled in the holes, and planted Gold of Ophir roses they had brought from Pennsylvania. The vines thrived on the unexpected bounty of the richness beneath them, and I remember great heaps of them in every backyard in Whittier, blazing like moons on fire, yellow, gold, pink—and in the shade. I'll always remember their lovely color.

—from the Introduction to *Growing Good Roses,* 1988

Into the Rose Garden

BY MICHAEL POLLAN

Once you have grown roses, you can begin to understand why people might project metaphors of social class onto them. Each bush itself forms a kind of social hierarchy. Beneath Madame Hardy's bud union is the rootstock of another, tougher variety— not a rose hybrid but a crude species rose, some hardy peasant stock that can withstand bad winters, but whose meager flowers interest no one. The prized hybrid is grafted onto the back of this anonymous rootstock, which performs all the hard labor for the rose, working the soil, getting its roots dirty so that the plant may bloom. The prickly shrub itself is not distinguished particularly, but it too is necessary to support the luxury of the bloom—its great mass of leaves manufactures the food, and its branches form the architecture without which flowering would not be possible. And the extravagant, splendid blooms, like true aristocrats, never seem to acknowledge the plant that supports them, or the fact that their own petals were once mere leaves. They comport themselves as though their beauty and station were god-given, transcendent.

You cannot discern in the bloom of a rose the work of the plant, the sacrifice of its chafer-eaten leaves, the stink of the manure in which it is rooted. Roots? Madame Hardy asks, ingenuously. What roots? But if Madame Hardy calls attention to her pedigree, Maiden's Blush, the alba I planted beside her in my garden, seems to press her sexuality on us. Her petals are more loosely arrayed than Madame Hardy's; less done up, almost unbuttoned. Her petals are larger, too, and they flush with the palest flesh pink toward the center, which itself is elusive, concealed in the multiplication of her labial folds. The blush of this maiden is not in her face only. Could I be imagining things? Well, consider some of the other names by which this rose is known: Virginale, Incarnata, La Séduisante, and Cuisse de Nymphe. This last is what the rose is called in France where, as Vita Sackville-West tells us, blooms that blush a particularly deep pink are given the "highly expressive name" of Cuisse de Nymphe Émue, which she demurs from translating. But there it is: the thigh of an aroused nymph.

No, Maiden's Blush is certainly not the kind of old lady I expected when I planted roses. Her concupiscence, in fact, has made me wonder if all the baggage with which the rose has been loaded down might be just a cover for these nymph thighs, for this unmistakable carnality. For though Maiden's Blush bears an especially provocative bloom, every one of the old roses I planted, and all the ones I've since seen and smelled, have been deeply sensuous in a way I wasn't prepared for. Compared to the chaste buds and modest scent of the modern roses, these old ones give freely of themselves. They flower all at once, in a single, climactic week. Their blooms look best fully opened, when their form is most intricate; explicit, yet still so deeply enfolded on themselves as to imply a certain inward mystery. And their various perfumes — ripe peaches, burnt almonds, young chardonnays, even musk — can be overpowering. More even than most floral scents, the fragrance of these roses is impossible to get hold of or describe —

it seems to short-circuit conscious thought, to travel in a straight line from nostril to brain stem. Inhale deeply the perfume of a bourbon rose and then try to separate out what is scent, what is memory, what is emotion; you cannot pull apart the threads that form this . . . this *what?*

By the time all my old roses had bloomed I had begun to think that maybe Marx has less to tell us about the world of roses than Freud. Certainly Freud would assume that anything we have invested with this much significance must exert some powerful sexual pull. I returned to my rose literature, and surely enough, the same rosarians whose prose had seemed to bristle with class consciousness now read to me as slightly sex-crazed. Would it be disrespectful to suggest that Graham Stuart Thomas, O.B.E., V.M.H., D.H.M., V.M.M., has a thing for old roses? Here is his full description of Madame Hardy: "There is just a suspicion of flesh pink in the half-open buds, emerging from their long calyces, and the flower open-cupped, rapidly becoming flat, the outer petals reflexing in a most beautiful manner, leaving the center almost concave, of pure white, with a small green eye . . . sumptuous and ravishing." The scent of Maiden's Blush reduces Sir Thomas to the rapturous ineffables of a trashy romance writer: her blooms are "intense, intoxicating, delicious . . . my senses have not yet found the means of conveying to my pen their qualities." Marie Louise, a rose raised at Malmaison in 1813, brings out the Humbert Humbert in him: "To lift up the leafy sprays and look steadily at the fully opened blooms is a revelation. . . ." I was beginning to understand why rosarians tend to be men. Men, and then of course Vita Sackville-West, who could certainly work herself up writing about old roses: "Rich they were, rich as a fig broken open, soft as a ripened peach, freckled as an apricot, coral as pomegranate, bloomy as a bunch of grapes . . ." Your opinion, Doctor Freud?

If the allure of old roses is in the frank sensuality of their blooms, then what are we to make of the development and eventual triumph of the modern hybrid tea? Maybe the Victorian middle class simply couldn't deal with the rose's sexuality. Perhaps what really happened in 1867 was a monumental act of horticultural repression. By transforming the ideal of rose beauty from the fully opened bloom to the bud, the Victorians took a womanly flower and turned her into a virgin—a venerated beauty when poised on the verge of opening, but quickly fallen after that.

As for the prized new trait of continual bloom, that too can be seen as a form of sublimation. For the hybrid roses don't give more bloom, really, they just parcel their blooms out over a longer period; they save and reinvest. So instead of abandoning herself to one great climax of bloom, the rose now doles out her blossoms one by one, always holding back, forever on the verge, never quite . . . finishing. The idea of a flower that never finishes would have struck the Elizabethans as perverse; one of the things they loved most about the rose was the way it held nothing back, the way it bloomed unreservedly and then was spent. But the Victorians bred this sexual rhythm out of the rose, subordinating it to the period's cult of virginity, as well as its new concepts of economy. From them we've inherited a girlish flower, pretty perhaps, but scrubbed to the point of scentlessness, no more alluring or sexually aware than a girl scout.

To look at a flower and think of sex—what exactly can this mean? Emerson wrote that "nature always wears the colors of the spirit," by which he meant that we don't see nature plain, only through a screen of human tropes. So in our eyes spring becomes youth, trees truths, and even the humble ant becomes a bighearted soldier. And certainly when we look at roses and see aristocrats, old ladies and girl scouts, or symbols of love and purity, we are projecting human categories onto them, saddling them with the burden of our metaphors.

But is there any other way to look at nature? Thoreau thought there was. He plumbed Walden Pond in winter in order to relieve nature of precisely this human burden—to "recover the long lost bottom of Walden Pond" from the local legends that held it bottomless. Thoreau was confident he could distinguish between nature (the pond, which he determined had a depth of exactly one hundred and two feet) and culture (the stories people told about its bottomlessness); he strove to drive a wedge between the two once and for all—to see the pond with a mind of winter: unencumbered, as it really was. "Let us settle ourselves, and work and wedge our feet downward through the mud and slush of opinion, and prejudice, and tradition, and delusion, and appearance, that alluvion which covers the globe . . . till we come to a hard bottom and rocks in place, which we can call *reality*, and say, This is . . ." The transcendentalists looked to nature as a cure for culture, but before it can exert its "sanative influence," we have first to scrape off the crust of culture that has formed over it.

This neat segregation of nature and culture gets complicated when you get to garden plants such as the rose, which perhaps begins to explain why Thoreau preferred swamps to gardens. For the rose not only wears the colors of our spirit, it *contains* them. Roses have been "cultivated" for so long, crossed and recrossed to reflect our ideals, that it is by now impossible to separate their nature from our culture. It is more than a conceit to suggest that Madame Hardy's elegance embodies something of the society that produced her, or that Graceland's slickness embodies something of ours. To a certain extent, the same holds true for all hybrid plants, but no other has received as much sustained attention from the hybridizer, that practitioner, in Shakespeare's words, of an "art [that] itself is nature." Thoreau could not have gotten what he wanted looking at a rose; the rose has been so heavily burdened with human "prejudice, and tradition, and delusion"—with human history—that by now there is no hard bottom to be found there. "The mud and slush of opinion" has been bred right into Dolly Parton; she's more a symptom of culture than a cure for it.

But if Dolly Parton suggests that our intercourse with nature will sometimes produce regrettable offspring, that doesn't necessarily mean we are better off with swamps. It is too late in the day—there are simply too many of us now—to follow Thoreau into the woods, to look to nature to somehow cure or undo culture. As important as it is to have swamps, today it is probably more important to learn how to mingle our art with nature in ways that culminate in a Madame Hardy rather than a Dolly Parton—in forms of human creation that satisfy culture without offending nature. The habit of bluntly opposing nature and culture has only gotten us into trouble, and we won't work ourselves free of this trouble until we have developed a more complicated and supple sense of how we fit into nature. I do not know what that sense might be, but I suspect that the rose, with its long, quirky history of give-and-take with man, can tutor it as well as, if not better than, Thoreau's unsullied swamp.

Even once we have recognized the falseness of the dichotomy between nature and culture, it is hard to break its hold on our minds and our language; look how often I fall back on its terms. Our alienation from nature runs deep. Yet even to speak in terms of a compromise between nature and culture is not quite right either, since it implies a distance between the two—implies that we are not part of nature. So many of our metaphors depend on this rift, on a too-easy sense of what is nature and what is "a color of the spirit." What we need is to confound our metaphors, and the rose can help us do this better than the swamp can.

That perhaps is what matters when we look at a rose blossom and think of sex. In my garden this summer, Maiden's Blush has flowered hugely, some of her blossoms flushed so deeply pink as to deserve the adjective *émue*. So what does it mean to look at these blossoms and think of sex? Am I thinking metaphorically? Well, yes and no. This flower, like all flowers, *is* a sexual organ. The uncultured bumblebee seems to find this bloom just as attractive as I do; he seems just as bowled over by its perfume. Yet I can't believe I gaze at the blossom in quite the same way he does. Its allure, for me, has to do with its resemblance to women—to "the thighs of an aroused nymph," about which I can assume he feels nothing. For this is a resemblance my species has bred, or selected, this rose to have. So is it imaginary? Merely a representation? (But what about the bee?! That's no representation he's pollinating.) Are we, finally, speaking of nature or culture when we speak of a rose (nature) that has been bred (culture) so that its blossoms (nature) make men imagine (culture) the sex of women (nature)?

It may be this sort of confusion that we need more of.

—from *Second Nature*, 1991

Horse-Chestnut Trees and Roses

BY JAMES SCHUYLER

Twenty-some years ago, I read Graham Stuart Thomas's
"Colour in the Winter Garden." I didn't plant
a winter garden, but the book led on to his
rose books: "The Old Shrub Roses," "Shrub Roses
of Today," and the one about climbers and ramblers.

By the corner of the arbor I planted the splendid
Nevada (a Spanish rose, Pedro Dot) and on the arbor
yellow Lawrence Johnston—I've never known
anyone who made a real success of that. Then
a small flowered rose (like a blackberry in flower),
whose name I forget, and then, oh loveliness, oh
glory, Mme. Alfred Carrière, white, with a faintest
blush of pink, and which will bloom even on a
north wall. I used to shave and gaze down into her—
morning kisses. The day Robert Kennedy died, a
green and evil worm crawled out of a bud. I killed
it, a gardening Sirhan Sirhan.

At the corner of the house Rosa Mutabilis fluttered
its single, changeable wings. My favorite, perhaps.

Then, in the border, along the south side of
the white house, Golden Wings (a patented rose —
did you know you can patent roses? Well, you can);
prickly, purplish Rose de Rescht; Souvenir
de la Malmaison (named by a Russian Grand Duke in
honor of the Empress Joséphine, Empress of Rosarians);
Mabel Morrison, lifting her blowsy white blooms
to the living-room windows.

The Georg Arends, whose silver-pink petals
uniquely fold into sharp points (or is Georg
my favorite?).

And darkly brooding Prince Camille de Rohan, on
which, out of a cloudless sky, a miraculous rain
once fell. (But I'm forgetting Gloire de Dijon,
Dean Hole's favorite rose.)

Then the smallest, most delicate, delectable
of all, Rose de Meaux. Alas, it pined away.

And elsewhere more: Rosa Gallica, the striped
and the pink, the Pembertons, Persian yellow,
and unforgettable cerise Zéphirine Drouhin.
And a gray rose, Reine des Violettes. Sweet-
brier, Mme. Pierre Oger, Variegata di Bologna,
"like raspberries and cream." And more,
whose names escape me.

I went by there Sunday last and they're gone, all gone, uprooted, supplanted by a hateful "foundation planting" of dinky conifers, some pointed, some squatty roundish. I put a curse on it and them.

On either side of the front walk there towered two old horse-chestnut trees. I loved their sticky, unfurling leaves, and when they bore their candles it was magic, breath-catching, eye-delighting. Cut down, cut down. What kind of man cuts down trees that took all those years to grow? I do not understand.

Oh, well, it's his house now, and I remove the curse, but not without a hope that Rose de Rescht and the rugosas gave him a good scratching. He deserved it.

But oh dear: I forgot the five Old China Monthly roses, and I always wish I'd planted Félicité et Perpétue—it's their names I like. And Climbing Lady Hillingdon.

(But the Garland grown as a fountain seemed somehow beyond me.)

There are roses and roses, always more roses. It's the horse-chestnut trees I mind.

—1993

Thoughts on Thistles

BY ROBIN LANE FOX

Thistles, Dr. Johnson might have said, are a symbol for Scotsmen and a food for donkeys. To gardeners, they mean sore fingers and tufts of down blowing into the strawberry bed, a prickly problem for the next year's croppers. But when I last walked across a stubble field, I looked at them closely and felt we had been unfair. Their prickly leaves spread outwards like a star which has fallen from heaven and been left lying face up on the ground. They have a bold shape and their prickles glisten in the rain. In a word, they have distinction. Something of this distinction may have rubbed off, at times too literally, on travellers to the Mediterranean in high summer and autumn. If you have never seen one of the thistly plateaux of Spain, Greece or Turkey, I recommend the descriptions of a thistle-landscape in the greatest contemporary Turkish novel, *Memed, My Hawk* by Yashar Kemal. There has never been a finer connoisseur of thistles in their element.

"The tallest thistles grow about a yard high, with many twigs decked with spiny flowers, five-pointed like stars, set among tough prickly thorns. There are hundreds of these flowers on each thistle. . . . In spring the thistles are an anaemic pale green. A light breeze can bend them to the earth. By midsummer, the first blue veins appear on the stems. Then the branches and the whole stem slowly turn a pale blue. Later, this blue grows steadily deeper till the whole boundless plain becomes a sea of the finest blue. If a wind blows towards sunset, the blue thistles ripple like the sea and rustle. As autumn approaches, the thistles dry up. The blue turns white and crackling sounds rise from them. Small milk-white snails, as big as buttons, cling to them in thousands, covering them like milk-white beads. The village is surrounded by a plain of thistles. There are no fields, no vineyards, no gardens. Only thistles."

Have I begun to persuade you or, like Kemal's characters, will you cut thistles down on sight, not even waiting for the drama of the second volume of the story? My favour for thistles is not, I trust, where we part company. I value daisies certainly, elder bushes possibly, but common thistles never, not even in a weed-ridden garden which we try to pass off as natural. Thistles are too prolific to be given a chance. But they have many more respectable relations. Catalogues conceal the similarities for fear of scaring customers away, but there are some rare and original plants, not difficult to grow, which have the same prickly habit and downy flowers as thistles themselves.

They come in all shapes and sizes, some as small as *Carduncellus rhaponticoides,* which sends out a flat rosette of stiff leaves as a setting for its lavender-mauve flowers like a tiny globe artichoke's. Others are as tall as the onopordon, that invaluable biennial with silver thistle-leaves which is 6 feet tall, like a huge pewter candlestick when given room to stand in isolation. Onopordum seed themselves from year to year, and can be bought in seed packets from firms as respectable as Burpee, Park Seed and Thompson and Morgan. Needless to say, they germinate very readily.

So does the annual Mary's Thistle, or Silybum, a superb hardy annual whose thistly dark green leaves are spotted with white, like drops of that ubiquitous liquid, the Virgin Mary's milk: Thompson and Morgan list and export these seeds which are almost fool-proof and admirable value in any garden-planting. They also sell the hooked and spiny *Morina longifolia* whose leaves are as nothing to its whorls of flowers, first white, then pink, then a blushing red when they have been fertilized. Like so many thistly plants, these flowers hold up nobly when dead and can be used very strikingly in a bowl of dried stems and flowers. The thistly globe artichoke is another friend of architectural planters: you can eat the buds, especially in the named Vert de Laon variety, and you can also enjoy the huge clumps of jagged grey-green leaves. At a lower level, you can pick the heads of the alpine thistle *Carlina acaulis,* which are disc-shaped and only a foot tall. They can be matched prettily with *Eryngium alpinum,* fluffiest and smartest of the smaller sea hollies, easily raised in dozens from seed. In Britain, Thompson and Morgan sells all these thistles and many eryngiums, including the superb grey-white biennial, *Eryngium giganteum,* named popularly after Miss Wilmott, a prickly Edwardian gardener who sowed it secretly in gardens she visited. In America, Park sells seed, conveniently, of both the eryngiums I have named.

So much for the outlines of the idea. Their angular shapes and prickles belong with the concrete yards and plate-glass windows of much modern building: their irregularity can enliven surroundings which are often left too flat. It is fashionable for gardeners to think of planting profusely and mixing their flowers in the abandon of the old cottage style. But it can be as subtle to plant too little as to plant too much. Style depends on the site and there are places where nostalgic, cottage profusion looks untidy. Gardens can be sharp and spiky as well as rose-embowered and honeysuckle-twined: there are corners and settings where thistles are not such an asinine taste after all.

—from *Variations on a Garden,* 1986

June 29–30

BY MAURICE MAETERLINCK

Brave old flowers! Wall-flowers, Gilly flowers, Stocks! For even as the field-flowers, from which a trifle, a ray of beauty, a drop of perfume, divides them, they have charming names, the softest in the language; and each of them, like tiny, art-less ex-votos, or like medals bestowed by the gratitude of men, proudly bears three or four.

 . . . Our language, I think, contains nothing that is better, more daintily, more affectionately named than these homely flowers. Here the word clothes the idea almost always with care, with light precision, with admirable happiness. It is like an ornate and transparent stuff that moulds the form which it embraces and has the proper shade, perfume and sound . . . their names depict them by equivalents and analogies which the greatest poets but rarely light upon.

—from *Old-fashioned Flowers,* 1907

Hydrangeas? Never!

BY ALLEN LACY

Show me a person without prejudice of any kind on any subject and I'll show you someone who may be admirably virtuous but is surely no gardener. Prejudice against people is reprehensible, but a healthy set of prejudices is a gardener's best friend. Gardening is complicated, and prejudice simplifies it enormously.

Plants can be divided into three basic sorts. There are those that only a madman could love. These include poison ivy (though it's pretty in the autumn), chickweed, crabgrass, wild onions, sticker burrs, and bull nettle — weeds that tempt most normal people to declare chemical war, no matter how deeply they may feel that Rachel Carson was on to something. Then there are those plants that only the perverse could dislike. Among garden flowers, these include bleeding heart, clematis, lilies, roses, and tulips. Among wildflowers, add butterfly weed, gentian, shooting stars, sunflowers, and, despite its name, toadflax.

But in between there are hundreds of flowering plants

about which some controversy is possible. No gardener, not even those few who still have lots of land and hosts of workers to do their bidding, can plant them all. Here, a little dose of prejudice comes to the rescue.

I have a friend who can't bear the sight of any flower whose stamens show. It may sound Victorian and quaint, but this antipathy makes her gardening exquisitely simple. At a blow, it excludes single peonies, daylilies, daisies, and dozens and dozens of other species from her consideration.

My own prejudices include celosias, purple alyssum, fancyleafed caladiums, annual salvias, gladiolas, and a surprisingly large number of other plants. Since my wife has a list that only partially overlaps mine, ordering seeds is for us much simpler than it might otherwise be.

But let me dwell for a moment on one plant I especially detest—the hydrangea, by which I mean the bushy ornamental sorts, not the tree and climbing kinds, which I admire. Where I live, a great many people adore hydrangeas. These folks are as inexplicable, to me, as those who enjoy eating haggis. There is a Hydrangea Trail that stretches more miles than I like to think about. People compete to win prizes for the best hydrangea. They call in photographers to have their pictures taken in front of their prized shrubs. They talk lovingly to total strangers about the hydrangeas they've got, the way some people talk about their grandchildren.

Not me. I just don't like them. I think they're a major mistake on the part of the evolutionary process. They seem best suited for the terraces of the fashionable spas of bygone days, not for home gardens. (I did like the hydrangeas that appeared on the terraces of the Lido hotel where Von Aschenbach stayed in the film *Death in Venice*. They added to the overall mood of decadence and obsession.)

Hydrangeas look artificial. I'd be hard put to tell the difference between a plastic one and a real one. And they are far too accommodating to people who have color schemes in mind for their gardens as well as their living rooms. Add lime to the soil, and the blossoms turn pink. Add aluminum sulphate, and they will go cobalt-blue. Add both, and they look confused. I like plants that have firm convictions about what color their flowers will be. Off with their heads!

I can imagine now a hundred devoted hydrangeaphiles advancing in protest, shouting, "Sir! Your negative feelings toward these plants are ill-considered and irrational. Unfair! Unfair!"

They would be absolutely correct, of course. I give reasons for not liking hydrangeas, but the dislike came first and the reasons afterward. Perhaps one day I'll decide that I like hydrangeas, after all, just as not long ago, after a lifetime of disaffection toward them, I decided that I really liked hostas. If and when that comes to pass with hydrangeas, I'll find new reasons to support my changed opinion.

—from *Home Ground: A Gardener's Miscellany,* 1984

Flowers I Love

BY MARY RUSSELL MITFORD

In truth, nothing can be more vulgar than my taste in flowers, for which I have a passion. I like scarcely any but the common ones. First and best I love violets, and primroses, and cowslips, and wood anemones, and the whole train of field flowers; then roses of every kind and colour, especially the great cabbage rose; then the blossoms of the lilac and laburnum, the horse-chestnut, the asters, the jasmine, and the honeysuckle; and to close the list, lilies of the valley, sweet peas, and the red pinks which are found in cottagers' gardens. This is my confession of faith.

—from a letter to William Elford, April 17, 1812

A Change of Plans

BY CHARLES KURALT

I have a friend, Granville Hall, who raises daffodils in Gloucester, Virginia. I feel lucky if I see him once every ten years, but he is the sort of man who doesn't let time and distance impede friendship. Nearly every summer he sends me a box of daffodil bulbs, old standbys and new hybrids, and I dutifully plant them in the fall in a grove of Connecticut maple trees, which I've come to think of as Granville's Woods.

I look forward to the October ritual. I take a sturdy bulb planter and a big bag of the right kind of fertilizer from the shed, and twist the twelve-month stiffness out of my gardening gloves, and spend a day or two filling in patches of ground where I haven't planted Granville's bulbs in years past. There is satisfaction in this. The bulbs don't need much attention from year to year, and that forest floor has become a pretty good daffodil show in the spring.

But I have not always been able to be there in the spring to enjoy it. One year, CBS News sent me off to Moscow in April for a summit conference, and another year to Beijing in the peak daffodil weeks. One of the frustrations of my job was not being able to say, "I'm sorry, I can't cover this cosmic event on the other side of the world, because I have to go watch my daffodils bloom."

Well, now I didn't have a job anymore. I was free to go watch my daffodils bloom, which, come to think of it, is everybody's reason for retiring—to take time to smell the flowers. And here I was, still driven by this immutable, rambling habit of mine, planning—on my own!—to be on the other side of the continent in daffodil season. Suddenly, the Monterey Peninsula didn't seem quite so crucial to my perfect year. In a perfect year, you ought to be free to change your mind.

Besides, Granville Hall had paid me a considerable compliment the previous fall. Into his annual shipment of daffodil bulbs —large yellow trumpets and double whites and tazetta hybrids, each labeled by name—he had tucked a paper bag sealed with staples containing two bulbs he obviously meant to be special. When I opened the bag, a label fell out. It said, "*Narcissus* Charles Kuralt." It took me a few minutes to realize it wasn't a joke. Granville had named a daffodil for me.

In a letter which came later, he said that in all his years breeding daffodils, this was the first cultivar he had ever registered. He sent along the certificate from the Royal Horticultural Society. He said he had raised the bulb from seed and had named it in honor of my impending retirement. In all the world, he said, there now existed just three "Charles Kuralt" daffodil bulbs. He wanted me to have two of them.

I had planted those two bulbs with special care in a pretty place, on a slope above a mill pond. They had been there gathering strength all winter. I calculated that their first shoots would appear toward the end of March, and that they should bloom in the third or fourth week of April. Narcissus, you know, was a youth who pined away in love for his own image in a pool of water and was turned into a flower. Now that Granville Hall had turned me into a flower, a wave of narcissism washed over me. I wanted to see myself as a daffodil. I decided Monterey Bay would still be there next year.

It was a lovely April in New York. I had acquired a writing room atop a building in midtown Manhattan and fixed it up with mahogany shelves and cabinets, shutters at the windows, and Oriental rugs on the floor. I installed the desk and chair I'd bought in New Orleans and arranged everything to resemble the library of a very small and down-at-the-heels men's club, just the effect I wanted. Now I went there to comport myself as a gentleman of leisure, to read at my desk when I wanted, and to type up my travel notes at an outdoor table on the planted terrace. I thought of this as reflection and meditation; once upon a time, I would have called it goofing off. I realized I was playing a role, but it was a role I was beginning to enjoy.

All the time, I was waiting for my daffodil to bloom. I knew a lot of hard work and good luck went into breeding a new daffodil, but I had no idea how much time and patience went into it, until I asked Granville Hall to tell me the details, and he responded with a letter from Gloucester. That's when I found out about the New Zealand butterfly.

Most of the daffodil varieties on file with the International Daffodil Registrar in London are the result of careful hybridizing — applying the pollen of one show-stopper bloom to the stigma of another — and keeping careful records of this cross-pollination for the five or six years it takes for a tiny seed to become a blooming bulb. But, as a flower, my own birth was unplanned. As we used to say down home in North Carolina, I was a love child.

Granville wrote, "I wish I could tell you that *n*. Charles Kuralt is the product of years of brilliant and strategic cross-pollination by a master of the trade. 'Tain't so.

"Your lovely namesake was conceived by a butterfly (or by an ant or a spider or a naive bee, or by the wind) among the plantings of 'Phil' Phillips at Otorohanga, new Zealand. The happy accident occurred in November of 1983.

"Phil Phillips, now deceased, was a world-famous hybridizer of 'Down Under' daffodils, and a generous man, to boot. Each spring (which ends in December down there), he would gather open (naturally) pollinated seeds from his faded blooms and send them to Dr. William Bender of Chambersburg, Pennsylvania. Dr. Bender nicknamed these shiny little black birdshots 'POPS'—Phillips Open Pollinated Seed—and, equally generously, offered them to others . . . *Narcissus* Charles Kuralt was among some 1,500 POPS I acquired from Dr. Bender and planted in the spring of 1984.

"(Incidentally, you will find that *n*. C. K. looks a great deal like 'Pop's Legacy,' with which Dr. Bender won 'Best Bloom in Show' at the National Show in King of Prussia, Pennsylvania. No small potato, that.)

"After they'd been two years in the seed bed, I transplanted all surviving seed (some don't germinate) of the POPS group to a regular row in my production field, where *n*. C. K. first bloomed in 1990. It caught my eye in the spring of '92, whereupon I dug it in June, and planted it in the fall in a T.L.C. bed in my side yard. An enthusiastic comment last March by my neighbor and resident expert inspired me to register it."

So, as a flower, I was the child of an unnamed mother and an unknown father, conceived in New Zealand, bred in tidewater Virginia, and now a resident of Connecticut. I was dying to know what I looked like. The possibilities, of course, were astronomical. Granville had told me that professional breeders who cross daffodil genes don't always, or even usually, obtain a pretty flower. So what could a butterfly (or ant or bee or spider) have accomplished by chance?

All I had to go on was a copy of Granville's application to the Royal Horticultural Society: "Seed parent: unknown. Pollen parent: unknown. Perianth: white, 53 mm. length, flat, spade-shaped, good overlap, good uniformity of shape. Corona: yellow, 53 mm. length, moderate funnel shape, flange concentric at 51 mm., notched about 5 mm. deep at 3 mm. intervals. Flowering season: early. Attributes: increases well, free flowering, good garden plant."

This sounded promising. I let my imagination wander. There was a new flower in the world! Perhaps all who saw it would be awe-struck and wish to have it for themselves. I didn't expect daffodil-mania to sweep the world like the tulip speculation of 1634; that year, a Dutch collector traded twelve sheep, eight pigs, four oxen, a bed, a suit of clothes, and a thousand pounds of cheese for a single Viceroy tulip bulb. But I had heard of high prices for daffodils. Three bulbs of a new variety, Will Scarlet, changed hands in 1899 for nearly a thousand dollars; a now-abundant daffodil named Fortune sold for seventy-five dollars a bulb when it was first introduced in 1923; and even King Alfred, which is now sold by the hundreds of tons each year and is the only daffodil name most people recognize, brought twenty or thirty dollars a bulb when it was a new variety. Maybe my namesake daffodil, which I was about to see for the first time, would become internationally coveted and make Granville Hall a rich man! Then I learned from Granville that there are more than twenty thousand named daffodils, and that another couple of hundred are added to the International Registry each year. This fact dimmed my dreams of fortune.

But it didn't dim the romance. It pleased me to think of those two bulbs in Connecticut giving forth their first pale green spikes to the sunshine. They were descendants of the first daffodil bulbs to make their way to Europe from Turkey in the Middle Ages, and of Wordsworth's daffodils in that poem I had to memorize in the sixth grade:

> Ten thousand saw I at a glance,
> Tossing their heads in sprightly dance.

Granville Hall told me those were very rudimentary daffodils Wordsworth saw in the English Lake Country. He wrote, "I wonder what he would compose if I took him to the Richmond show next spring?"

For modern breeding has changed the shapes and colors of daffodils and given the gardens and meadows of the world a variety beyond anything the old poet could have imagined two hundred years ago. The old, well-remembered flowers have contributed some of their finest qualities to hundreds of variations. Granville wrote, "All of the red, orange, and primrose in any daffodil anywhere in this world came from that little ring of red in the eye of *n*. Poeticus Recurvus (Old Pheasant's Eye)."

So I didn't go to California. I did some reading and writing and relaxing, and then I went to Connecticut. I was there on the morning the first *Narcissus* Charles Kuralt opened to the world. Some daffodils are showy and assertive. Some are pert. This one was delicate and refined. From the midst of its creamy white petals arose a trumpet of pale yellow with a feathery lemon-yellow fringe. The flower faced the sun demurely, but with what I thought was a certain confidence. Well, it seemed to say, here I am. What do you think? I thought it was beautiful, and not quite like any other daffodil I'd ever seen.

Each bulb yielded two blooms. Each of the four flowers was perfect. Several times each day, I walked to the knoll where they were growing to make sure they were all right. When I had to return to New York, I cut them and drove them home with me. They rode in a glass of water wedged into the passenger seat. I stopped for gas at a place where they still clean your windshield, and the guy said, "Nice flowers." I wanted to tell him the whole story, of course. But all I said was, "Thanks."

When you leave your job after a long time in the public eye, everybody wants to have a dinner and give you a plaque or a scroll. . . . But I didn't know what narcissism was until I beheld my own narcissus.

Plaques tarnish. Scrolls fade. But those daffodil bulbs will divide and multiply. Within a year or two, I'll be able to give a couple of bulbs to each of my daughters. If they plant them and care for them, those will divide in turn and yield bulbs for my grandchildren. With a little luck, the flower named Charles Kuralt will appear from the earth to bloom in the spring long years after the man of the same name is gone.

I guess that's not exactly immortality, but it's as close as I will ever get.

—from *Charles Kuralt's America*, 1995

The Bean-Field

BY HENRY DAVID THOREAU

My beans, the length of whose rows, added together, was seven miles already planted, were impatient to be hoed, for the earliest had grown considerably before the latest were in the ground; indeed they were not easily to be put off. What was the meaning of this so steady and self-respecting, this small Herculean labor, I knew not. I came to love my rows, my beans, though so many more than I wanted. They attached me to the earth, and so I got strength like Antaeus. But why should I raise them? Only Heaven knows. This was my curious labor all summer,—to make this portion of the earth's surface, which had yielded only cinque-foil, blackberries, johnswort, and the like, before, sweet wild fruits and pleasant flowers, produce instead this pulse. What shall I learn of beans or beans of me? I cherish them, I hoe them, early and late I have an eye to them; and this is my day's work. It is a fine broad leaf to look on. My auxiliaries are the dews and rains which water this dry soil, and what fertility is in the soil itself, which for the most part is lean and effete. My enemies are worms, cool days, and most of all woodchucks. The last have nibbled for me a quarter of an acre clean. But what right had I to oust johnswort and the rest, and break up their ancient herb garden? Soon, however, the remaining beans will be too tough for them, and go forward to meet new foes. . . .

I planted about two acres and a half of upland; and as it was only about fifteen years since the land was cleared, and I myself had got out two or three cords of stumps, I did not give it any manure; but in the course of the summer it appeared by the arrowheads which I turned up in hoeing, that an extinct nation had already dwelt here and planted corn and beans ere white men came to clear the land, and so, to some extent, had exhausted the soil for this very crop.

Before yet any woodchuck or squirrel had run across the road, or the sun had got above the shrub oaks, while all the dew was on, though the farmers warned me against it,—I would advise you to do all your work if possible while the dew is on,—I began to level the ranks of haughty weeds in my bean-field and throw dust upon their heads. Early in the morning I worked barefooted, dabbling like a plastic artist in the dewy and crumbling sand, but later in the day the sun blistered my feet. There the sun lighted me to hoe beans, pacing slowly backward and forward over that yellow gravelly upland, between the long green rows, fifteen rods, the one end terminating in a shrub oak copse where I could rest in the shade, the other in a blackberry field where the green berries deepened their tints by the time I had made another bout. Removing the weeds, putting fresh soil about the bean stems, and encouraging this weed which I had sown, making the yellow soil express its summer thought in bean leaves and blossoms rather than in wormwood and piper and millet grass, making the earth say beans instead of grass,—this was my daily work. . . .

It was a singular experience that long acquaintance which I cultivated with beans, what with planting, and hoeing, and harvesting, and threshing, and picking over, and selling them,—the last was the hardest of all,—I might add eating, for I did taste. I was determined to know beans. When they were growing, I used to hoe from five o'clock in the morning till noon, and commonly spent the rest of the day about other affairs. Consider the intimate and curious acquaintance one makes with various kinds of weeds,—it will bear some iteration in the account, for there was no little iteration in the labor,—disturbing their delicate organizations so ruthlessly, and making such invidious distinction with his hoe, levelling whole ranks of one species, and sedulously cultivating another. That's Roman wormwood,—that's pigweed,—that's sorrel,—that's piper-grass,—have at him, chop him up, turn his roots upward to the sun, don't let him have a fibre in the shade, if you do he'll turn himself t'other side up and be as green as a leek in two days. A long war, not with cranes, but with weeds, those Trojans who had sun and rain and dews on their side. Daily the beans saw me come to their rescue armed with a hoe, and thin the ranks of their enemies, filling up the trenches with weedy dead. Many a lusty crest-waving Hector, that towered a whole foot above his crowding comrades, fell before my weapon and rolled in the dust.

Those summer days which some of my contemporaries devoted to the fine arts in Boston or Rome, and others to contemplation in India, and others to trade in London or New York, I thus, with the other farmers of New England, devoted to husbandry.

—from *Walden*, 1854

The Day of the Living Dead

BY PATRICIA THORPE

However sad it is when something dies, it can be even sadder when something doesn't. At least death is final—you can dig up the corpse and plant something else. But how much more wretched are those plants that clearly don't want to live, but don't want to die. These are plants that barely start to leaf out by July, are actually brave enough to make new growth by Labor Day, then turn black at the first touch of frost. These are plants that after two years of feeble growth suddenly produce a suspiciously vigorous set of shoots that have leaves, flowers, or fruits utterly unlike what you originally planted. And how about those shrubs that spray out scrawny arms four or five feet high but only bloom at the bottom three inches? Or those plants that retreat rather than advance in size?

For a few years you may admire the will to live that keeps a plant growing when it is clearly miserable. Perhaps you even congratulate yourself on your superior cultivation that makes it persist against all odds. These plants are like the enormous tortoises in zoos—they aren't really living; they are just taking an extraordinarily long time to die.

After killing off a number of plants inadvertently, it may be hard to face horticultural euthanasia. It is easy to stall: maybe this year will be milder; maybe it needs more time to settle in (perhaps ten more years?). But the misfortune of these mistakes goes beyond a small blot on your landscape. These sad relics are the lessons you are refusing to learn. By keeping them around, you are insisting that you are right: that you don't really live in Zone 4; that your soil *is* acid enough for blueberries; that roses don't need full sun; that taxodiums shouldn't mind a dry spell or two. It is true that some plants are hardier as they get older, and if you get them through the first crucial years you may have success. But after four or five years you have to make an assessment of your selections and stop nursing along specimens that long for *requiescat in pace*. You will be amazed what a lift it will give your whole garden to be rid of these ghosts. . . .

In the early days we mostly killed easy plants, plants we had every right to expect to grow. We can go back and grow them again—this time, perhaps, with success. But now most of us want to go beyond the plants that everyone can grow. We begin to long for plants we have never seen, plants with no common name, plants that have never ventured into our climate. Some of these experiments may broaden our horticultural horizons, but they may also expand our R.I.P. list.

Death is a forceful teacher of the limits of our own knowledge and it has shaped our gardens as we have learned from it. As we garden more, we discover that death has lost some of its terror, at least as it pertains to plants. We no longer feel the paralyzing remorse that once marked the discovery of every corpse, that made us swear we would never lift another shovelful of dirt. We know that there are plants we have no right to expect to grow, but at times we cheat the odds, or the climate, or conventional wisdom, and succeed. In those moments we feel like the heroes in fairy tales who gamble with death and win. We can flirt with disaster; we can sport with mortality. We may lose interest in plants with too tenacious a hold on life and court instead the young Werthers of the seed lists—*Eritrichium nanum, Androsace helvetica, Campanula arvatica*—plants so bent on their own destruction that even having a good-size corpse is a badge of distinction. Death may eventually have the last word, but until then we may learn to live with it.

—from *Growing Pains: Time and Change in the Garden,* 1994

GARDEN VARIETY

Lord Illingworth: The Book of Life begins
with a man and woman in a garden.

Mrs. Allonby: It ends with Revelations.

—*OSCAR WILDE, 1893*

Cuttings
(later)

by THEODORE ROETHKE

This urge, wrestle, resurrection of dry sticks,
Cut stems struggling to put down feet,
What saint strained so much,
Rose on such lopped limbs to a new life?

I can hear, underground, that sucking and sobbing,
In my veins, in my bones I feel it,—
The small waters seeping upward,
The tight grains parting at last.
When sprouts break out,
Slippery as fish,
I quail, lean to beginnings, sheath-wet.

—from *The Lost Son and Other Poems,* 1948

Magenta the Maligned

BY LOUISE BEEBE WILDER

Magenta is so universally despised and shunned. Not only is it deprived of its proper foils, but it is nearly always set down beside those colours surest to bring out its worst side. I am very fond of this colour as worn by flowers and have taken some trouble to bring it into harmony with its surroundings. Combative it is, but to be won; fastidious as to its associations, but gentle and beautiful when considered. Surely any one who has seen the sumptuous rim of colour following the banks of the Hudson River and its tributary streams on certain sections where the Rose Loosestrife, a flower of the purest magenta, has naturalized itself, will not deny the possibility of beauty in the use of this colour. Besides the Loosestrife many of the finest hardy plants garb themselves in the maligned hue, but in all my gardening experience I have met only one person who confessed admiration for this colour and I have come across but one garden writer who boldly put down in print his admiration for it. Indeed nearly every writer upon garden topics pauses in his praise of other flower colours to give the despised one a rap in passing. Mr. Bowles writes of "that awful form of floral original sin, magenta"; Miss Jekyll calls it "malignant magenta"; and Mrs. Earl, usually so sympathetic and tender toward all flowers, says that even the word magenta, seen often in the pages of her charming book, "makes the black and white look cheap," and again "if I could turn all magenta flowers pink or purple, I should never think further about garden harmony, all other colours would adjust themselves."

In the thoughtlessness of colour arrangement that prevailed in the gardens of our grandmothers, magenta was recklessly handled—so many sweet and willing flowers wore the now despised hue—but no one felt the horror of such great masses of magenta Phlox and Tiger Lilies, of magenta Foxgloves and scarlet Sweet William that I remember in the charming box-bordered garden of my grandparents in Massachusetts. But now, with this new vision of ours for colour harmony, there is no reason why we should, on account of the past sins of our forefathers and the present sinning of our nurserymen in miscalling it, banish this rich and distinctive colour with all the fine plants that it distinguishes, without some effort to provide for it the proper foils to fully develop its beauty. . . .

It is the custom to despise magenta. It is hustled out of our gardens and out of our consciousness and no one has eyes to see the imperial scarf of magenta Phlox that stoops to bind the dusty roadside, or the riot of tender colour in the neglected cottage dooryard where Petunias have sown and resown themselves and flutter about the gray and rotting porch and squeeze through the gray and rotting palings of the fence in exquisite harmony with the weathered wood. . . .

I do not deny that there are poor and wishy-washy tones

of magenta and that these are not desirable; but where the colour is frank and pure and used with a right intermingling of green and other soft friendly hues, there is none more beautiful and distinctive.

—from *Colour in My Garden,* 1918

Scent and the Gardener

BY STEPHEN LACEY

Scent is the most potent and bewitching substance in the gardener's repertory and yet it is the most neglected and the least understood. The faintest waft is sometimes enough to induce feelings of hunger or anticipation, or to transport you back through time and space to a long-forgotten moment in your childhood. It can overwhelm you in an instant or simply tease you, creeping into your consciousness slowly and evaporating almost the moment it is detected. Each fragrance, whether sweet or spicy, light or heavy, comes upon you in its own way and evokes its own emotional response.

But although scent adds such a pleasurable layer to our enjoyment, few of us treat it at all seriously—it remains an optional extra in the composition of a garden, rather than an integral part to be managed and manipulated for maximum impact. We may have the odd scented plant here and there, but we rarely plan for specific effects or pursue deliberate themes. Often we do not even realize a plant is scented until we acquire it, for catalogues and reference books frequently make no mention of scent in their descriptions. And even if they do, it is generally as an aside which gives no clue of the precise flavour.

There are of course many good reasons why we fail to use scent effectively. First, although the nose can be highly sensitive, we seldom take the trouble to identify what we are smelling and to put our impressions into words. Consequently, we have not developed a means of comparing and classifying scents and our vocabulary for describing them is very primitive: the adjective "sweet" encompasses everything from rose petals to five pound notes and dollar bills.

It has been suggested that this lazy attitude to scents has come about because the olfactory sense is no longer crucially important to us in our day-to-day life. For lower animals, scent is a means of navigating (salmon follow odour trails back to their spawning grounds), locating food (most mammals smell food before they see it), sensing danger (all hunters have to approach their prey downwind), establishing territory (many animals spray their surroundings with urine or rub their scent glands), deterring (skunk), communicating (deer produce an alarm scent; bees inform each other of the location of nectar sources; and many animals read tribal and social status from each other's scent) and advertising sexual ripeness.

Although we no longer rely on our sense of smell for survival, we do make use of it constantly: the flavour of our food and drink comes from our sense of smell. If you hold your nose while you eat and drink, you only receive general impressions of sweetness, sourness, bitterness and saltiness through the taste buds in the mouth. It is because of this close relationship between taste and smell, and because most of our smelling is done through our mouth, that when we do attempt to describe a scent, it is so often in terms of foods: lemon, honey, mint, blackcurrant, raspberry, pineapple, curry, chocolate, vanilla, coconut, clove and almond.

To make description and comparison even more difficult, each of us has different levels of sensitivity to scents and each of us reacts to them in different ways. Some people catch the most elusive flavours, while others have a relatively weak sense of smell and appreciate only the sledgehammer scents. Darkhaired people are said to be more sensitive than fair-haired people (because the olfactory mucous membrane is slightly pigmented) and smoking also impairs your sensitivity. Most of us have favourite scents and scents we detest; sometimes our reactions are inexplicable, sometimes they are associated with places, people and events in our past.

Fragrances are themselves highly complex. They consist of a number of compounds that ebb and flow according to weather conditions and the life cycle of the plants. They can change and disappear from one moment to the next and can be quite different when savoured at close range than at a distance. So we can never exactly predict how they will taste or how we are going to react to them. But these uncertainties make the use of scent a more challenging and intriguing subject for the gardener. They should certainly not put us off trying to understand and manage it. As Gertrude Jekyll wrote, each step in gardening is a step into a "delightful Unknown" and we should never be daunted by "groping ignorance."

—from *Scent in Your Garden*, 1991

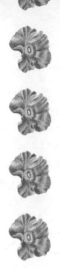

The Changing Rose, the Enduring Cabbage

BY KATHARINE S. WHITE

Fragrance, whether strong or delicate, is a highly subjective matter, and one gardener's perfume is another gardener's stink. My tastes are catholic. I very much like the pungent late-summer flowers—the marigolds, calendulas, and chrysanthemums, even the old-fashioned single nasturtiums that have not been prettied up by the hybridizers. These ranker autumn flowers, dome of whose pungency comes from the foliage, are what Louise Beebe Wilder, in her book *The Fragrant Path* (1932), calls "nose twisters"; the very word "nasturtium" means "nose twister" in Latin. It is my habit to keep two little vases filled with small flowers on our living-room mantelpiece all summer; by September, these are often filled with nose twisters—French marigolds, miniature Persian carpet zinnias, calendulas, and a few short sprays from the tall heleniums, all in the tawny and gold shades of autumn. But to some people the aromatic scents of these flowers and their leaves are unbearable. In fact, one friend of mine cannot tolerate them at all, and her pretty nose will wrinkle with disgust when she is in the room with them. If I know she is coming to the house in September, I hastily change my bouquets to the softer tones and sweeter scents of the late-flowering verbenas, annual phlox, and petunias.

I know next to nothing about fragrance. A year of trying to learn about it has left me as ignorant as ever, beyond a few simple facts that everybody knows, such as that a moist, warm day with a touch of sun will bring out fragrance, that hot sun and droughts can destroy it, and that rain will draw out the good chlorophyll scents of grass and foliage. The commonest complaint one hears today from the amateur gardener is that modern flowers, particularly roses, are losing their fragrance, thanks to the hybridizers' emphasis on form and colour, and it had seemed to me, too, that many flowers smell less sweet than they used to. Sweet peas: the ones I grow are sweet, of course, but I remember them as sweeter still in my aunts' flower garden of long ago. Iris: it is rare to find a fragrant flower among the hybrids we now grow on our terrace, but a gardening friend with a particularly alert nose remembers the old-fashioned "flag lilies" of his childhood as very fragrant. Lilacs: the common single farmyard lilac for me has the headiest spring scent of all, and some of the double modern French hybrids are said to be as fragrant, yet the double lilacs we grow here are distinctly less sweet than our common lilacs (*Syringa vulgaris*), probably because one of their ancestors was the only wild lilac that has no scent at all. Pansies: oh, the list of lost sweet smells could go on and on.

These vexing doubts have given me courage to write around, asking questions of the scientists and horticulturists and commercial growers whom I dared to bother with my inquiries. A few of them have answered helpfully, a few evasively, but most of them mysteriously. The only consensus I can gather is that fragrance is not a strong incentive among the growers and breeders. Colour and form and hardiness are the thing, because that is what the public demands.

—from *Onward and Upward in the Garden*, 1979

I Remember, I Remember

BY THALASSA CRUSO

For many people the scent of certain plants can revive memories with a vividness that nothing else can equal, for the sense of smell can be extraordinarily evocative, bringing back pictures as sharp as photographs of scenes that had left the conscious mind. Whenever I come in contact with flowering ivy, I find I have almost total recall of a very early ground plan of my parents' first country garden. That particular garden was later entirely redesigned as my parents developed new tastes, and when I think back consciously about how and where they managed their plants, I always visualize the details of the later stage, which I knew far longer and also when I was getting interested in plants. But the instant some dormant lobe in my mind is retriggered by the pungent, heavy, almost unpleasant smell of flowering ivy, I suddenly see with great clarity the first garden including minute details—with which I sometimes confound my brother, who does not possess this visual sense of total recall. Above all, I remember the source of the ivy memory jogger: a small peat shed, my special hiding place during the early years of our occupation of that house, which had to be taken down around about the time I was nine years old. It was so weighted down with luxuriant ivy that it was judged unsafe.

In New England, except for the Baltic variety, ivy rarely flowers; the harsh winters kill it back too hard. For ivy must scramble to a certain height above the ground and reach a fixed stage of leaf maturity before it will set a bud. And it was not until I recently brushed against a flowering spray, in a warmer section of the country where ivy flourishes all too happily, that I again realized that the old nerve still existed and was only waiting to be plucked. Tree ivies, by which I do not mean the modern hybrid of ivy and a fatsia, called fatshedera, but true ivy grown into a standard form, are no longer popular. They used to be very fashionable and were used as what then were called "dot," or to us "accent," plants to give height to an area planted entirely in low annuals. True ivy standards are now hard to come by partly because they take time and patience and a good deal of room for winter storage, but also because they can be made only from cuttings of ivy that are mature enough to flower, and rooted cuttings of old wood are always hard to strike. I have no passionate wish to possess a tree or standard ivy; I suspect I would have just the same trouble with it as I have with the juvenile trailing form we all grow. But I had almost forgotten their very existence until that pungent smell also reawakened the visual memory of my grandfather's long parterre beds with the ivies standing like sentinels at regular intervals along it.

Unlike many people, I am not all that enthusiastic about roses. I love climbing roses and grow a lot of them as well as old-fashioned rambler roses, but in a very simple style scrambling among the trees or flinging themselves over stone walls where they give no trouble except to require an occasional thorny cutting out. But I am not much interested in rose gardens, and I dislike the heavy scent of roses indoors. I can rationalize this by saying that roses in this country take too much care and are prone to too many diseases, while roses indoors shatter irritatingly fast, all of which is perfectly true. But I think the truth of my indifference has deeper roots. The family rose garden, which was my father's delight, was always at its superlative best in June, the time of year when vital examinations were held in English schools. I was rather a ten o'clock scholar and used to leave a great deal undone until the last possible moment. Then I used to pace around and around the circular rose garden, which was a little set off to one side and therefore a quiet place, feverishly cramming for the upcoming examinations. The scent and sight of roses have therefore an association of tension in the back of my mind, and this is probably the real reason for my lack of interest in them.

And I find this childhood association syndrome exists in all sorts of gardening matters. Our country garden is surrounded by tall hedges in which we battle the twin plagues of bittersweet and Japanese honeysuckle. In spite of our counterattacks both plants are going to outlast us, and where the bittersweet is concerned I find I have ambivalent feelings about cutting out the fruiting strands even though they are doing their best to strangle us. As a child I used to hunt for bittersweet berries in the hedges along the chalk downs. Those two-tone sprays that I now cut out were there a trophy to be proudly carried home, for bittersweet is not the nuisance in England that it has become in some areas here. I am sure it is a relic of this feeling that leads me to emphasize the importance of the berries for the bird population and turn my fiercest efforts against the unberried strands.

I deplore the pythonlike grip with which the Japanese honeysuckle strangles everything within reach, but I love the elusive fragrance with which it envelopes the country garden at this season. To me that epitomizes everything we enjoy about this slightly ramshackle but deeply loved garden, and that same scent, it seems, is apparently going to affect my children just as ivy keeps its hold over me. For recently standing on the porch in the evening with honeysuckle perfuming the air, a visiting daughter who now lives where this vine does not grow suddenly remarked that to her the smell of honeysuckle would always mean that school was out and the endless sunny summer had begun. She had forgotten the sensation until that very moment.

Scents bring memories, and many memories bring nostalgic pleasure. We would be wise to plan for this when we plant a garden.

—from *To Everything There Is a Season*, 1973

The Feline Touch

BY BEVERLEY NICHOLS

A garden without cats, it will be generally agreed, can scarcely deserve to be called a garden at all. There is something dead about a lawn which has never been shadowed by the swift silhouette of a dancing kitten, and much of the magic of the heather beds would vanish if, as we bent over them, there was no chance that we might hear a faint rustle among the blossoms, and find ourselves staring into a pair of sleepy, green eyes. . . .

The harm done by cats is negligible. Naturally, if a gardener is so foolish as to leave seed-boxes all over the place, he is asking for trouble; cats have been brought up by humans to regard these utensils as powdering closets, and as such they promptly use them. To fail to do so, they doubtless imagine, would be discourteous. And if the gardener leaves a window of the greenhouse ajar, and if a cat, making its tour of inspection, observes a patch of sunlight falling across a row of pots, the cat can hardly be blamed for jumping in, and curling up among the pots to bask in the warm glow that pervades them. He may—though rarely—knock one over; but the sheer delight of finding a cat in a greenhouse at all is more than adequate compensation for so trifling a mishap. What combination of circumstances could be more charming, more spiritually therapeutic? One opens the door and breaths in the scent of the leaves and the petals—the bittersweet tang of the geraniums and the moss-like fragrance of the hanging ferns—and then one suddenly observes a small black bundle, stretched across the skirting in an attitude of total abandon, with the petal of a begonia stuck to the end of its tail. The paws are lazily thrown back in a gesture of allurement, and as one bends down, a green eye opens and a tail twitches, very slightly, acknowledging one's caresses but also indicating that for the moment they are not essential.

—from *Garden Open Tomorrow*, 1968

A Mass of Sooty, Shapeless Slime

BY CELIA THAXTER

It seems to me the worst of all the plagues is the slug, the snail without a shell. He is beyond description repulsive, a mass of sooty, shapeless slime, and he devours everything. He seems to thrive on all the poisons known; salt and lime are the only things that have power upon him, at least the only things I have been able to find so far. But salt and lime must be used very carefully, or they destroy the plant as effectually as the slug would do. Every night, while the season is yet young, and the precious growths just beginning to make their way upward, feeling their strength, I go at sunset and heap along the edge of the flower beds air-slaked lime, or round certain most valuable plants a ring of the same,—the slug cannot cross this while it is fresh, but should it be left a day or two it loses its strength, it has no more power to burn, and the enemy may slide over it unharmed, leaving his track of slime. On many a solemn midnight have I stolen from my bed to visit my cherished treasures by the pale glimpses of the moon, that I might be quite sure the protecting rings were still strong enough to save them, for the slug eats by night, he is invisible by day unless it rains or the sky be overcast. He hides under every damp board or in any nook of shade, because the sun is death to him. I use salt for his destruction in the same way as the lime, but it is so dangerous for the plants, I am always afraid of it. Neither of these things must be left about them when they are watered lest the lime or salt sink into the earth in such quantities as to injure the tender roots. I have little cages of fine wire netting which I adjust over some plants, carefully heaping the earth about them to leave no loophole through which the enemy may crawl, and round some of the beds, which are inclosed in strips of wood, boxed, to hold the earth in place, long shallow troughs of wood are nailed and filled with salt to keep off the pests. Nothing that human ingenuity can suggest do I leave untried to save my beloved flowers! Every evening at sunset I place lime and salt about my pets, and every morning remove it before I sprinkle them at sunrise. The salt dissolves of itself in the humid sea air and in the dew, so around those for whose safety I am most solicitous I lay rings of pasteboard on which to heap it, to be certain of doing the plants no harm. Judge, reader, whether all this requires strength, patience, perseverance, hope! It is hard work beyond a doubt, but I do not grudge it, for great is my reward. Before I knew what to do to save my garden from the slugs, I have stood at evening rejoicing over rows of fresh emerald leaves just springing in rich lines along the beds, and woke in the morning to find the whole space stripped of any sign of green, as blank as a board over which a carpenter's plane has passed.

In the thickest of my fight with the slugs some one said to me, "Everything living has its enemy; the enemy of the slug is the toad. Why don't you import toads?"

I snatched at the hope held out to me, and immediately wrote to a friend on the mainland, "In the name of the Prophet,

Toads!" At once a force of only too willing boys was set about the
work of catching every toad within reach, and one day in June a
boat brought a box to me from the far-off express office. A piece
of wire netting was nailed across the top, and upon the earth with
which it was half filled, reposing among some dry and dusty green
leaves, sat three dry and dusty toads, wearily gazing at nothing. Is
this all, I thought, only three! Hardly worth sending so far. Poor
creatures, they looked so arid and wilted, I took up the hose and
turned upon them a gentle shower of fresh cool water, flooding the
box. I was not prepared for the result! The dry, baked earth heaved
tumultuously; up came dusky heads and shoulders and bright eyes
by the dozen. A sudden concert of liquid sweet notes was poured
out on the air from the whole rejoicing company. It was really
beautiful to hear that musical ripple of delight. I surveyed them
with eager interest as they sat singing and blinking together. "You
are not handsome," I said, as I took a hammer and wrenched off
the wire cover that shut them in, "but you will be lovely in my
sight if you will help me to destroy mine enemy"; and with that I
turned the box on its side and out they skipped into a perfect paradise of food and shade. All summer I came upon them in different parts of the garden, waxing fatter and fatter till they were as
round as apples. In the autumn baby toads no larger than my
thumb nail were found hopping merrily over the whole island.
There were sixty in that first importation; next summer I received
ninety more. But alas! small dogs discover them in the grass and
delight to tear and worry them to death, and the rats prey upon
them so that many perish in that way; yet I hope to keep enough
to preserve my garden in spite of fate.

In France the sale of toads for the protection of gardens is
universal, and I find under the head of "A Garden Friend," in a
current newspaper, the following item:—

"One is amused, in walking through the great Covent Garden Market, London, to find toads among the commodities offered

for sale. In such favor do these familiar reptiles stand with English market gardeners that they readily command a shilling apiece. . . . The toad has indeed no superior as a destroyer of noxious insects, and as he possesses no bad habits and is entirely inoffensive himself, every owner of a garden should treat him with utmost hospitality. It is quite worth the while not only to offer any simple inducements which suggest themselves for rendering the premises attractive to him, but should he show a tendency to wander away from them, to go so far as to exercise a gentle force in bringing him back to the regions where his services may be of the greatest utility."

—from *An Island Garden,* 1894

Dust to Dust: Undertakings in the Garden

BY PATTI HAGAN

For nine years I have been the super of a city garden and now I know for sure: No two denizens read a city garden the same way. As for one's own, you don't really know how your garden's going over until the day you hear the folks next door refer to "that jungle"; until you've sent Thelonious Monk, the rooster you'd rescued from full-moon ceremonies at the local voodoo parlor, up the river to be with some hens near Sing Sing, and the selfsame neighbors express dismay at his *absence*—whereas the lawyer two doors down had phoned daily to ascertain your long-term intentions in re "*that* rooster" whose crowing was wrecking his sleeping. But I did not know what the upstairs folks in the brownstone across the street thought until the night this spring they phoned about my garden, at 10 P.M.

These people had wanted to visit when the clematis-rose-peony-iris ensemble peaked, so I assumed they were making an appointment for the blooming weekend. Not exactly. They wanted to arrange an undertaking. "You see," my neighbor explained, "my husband's science class hatched these Pekin ducks from eggs as a school project a month ago. He brought two home for our six-year-old daughter, and they'd learned to swim in the bathtub, diving for guppies and goldfish. But this afternoon one of them, Funny, fell off the deck and died on the fire escape next door. My Jamaican neighbors didn't know there was a dead duck out there 'til I went over. The girl said, 'That duck's going to fly away. You just have to fix its wings.' But what was broken was its neck. I feel like a murderer and my daughter is very upset—and—could we bury our dead duck in your garden? Right now? I remember you said you had buried your dog there."

I recalled one day on the street having told this neighbor, who was musing about a final resting place for the elderly family dog, that four years ago, on a crisply beautiful spring day, my golden retriever, Thurber, had been put to sleep out back beside the blue columbine patch and that the kindly veterinarian had allowed Thurber to stay in the garden. "It's not legal," he had said, "but if you'll promise to give him a good Jewish burial—before sundown today—O.K." The six-year-old girl next door, who'd been questioning my gardening all along and had observed Thurber's passing through the chain-link-and-wisteria fence, thought things over for a few days and then asked: "If you water Thurber, will he turn into a plant?" (Thurber turned into a white birch, *Betula papyrifera*).

There was room for the duck between the white birch and a non-running bamboo, *Sinarundinaria nitida,* recently arrived from California. However, since my garden is intensely densely planted and by 10 P.M. visibility is low even with fireflies and the all-night burglar light of the people over the back fence, I proposed burial in the A.M. All the same, I wondered if it had occurred to my neighbor to ask her landlord, resident downstairs, if she might bury the duck in his all-ivy Skinner Box–style yard? Yes, the thought had occurred, but her landlord had AIDS and despite AZT had been hospitalized several times already. "I can't ask him about burying a dead duck— or even talk to him about anything to do with death." (And besides, the man hated flowers.)

Well, had she thought of asking the woman two houses down, who *likes* flowers and is a gardener? "I'm sure she'd freak out. Her garden is very orderly, very tidy, it has a *lawn* . . . I just wouldn't feel comfortable asking to disrupt that garden to bury a duck." Which is why my garden had come to mind. Not only was there already a golden retriever in it but, my neighbor observed, "your garden is so wild."

A little after eight the next morning she crossed the street carrying a shoebox with the deceased duck and a bag of lime borrowed from the gardener with the ruly garden. Funny was interred midway between the Thurber birch and the new bamboo. We covered the downy yellow duckling with a sprinkling of lime and a pickup potpourri of rose petals (Gloire des Mousseux, Jacques Cartier, Climbing Cecile Brunner, Golden Showers), the last fantastical black and blue parrot tulips, foxglove bugles, catalpa bells, bleeding heart lockets and clematis.

A while later my neighbor's daughter came to pay her last respects and lay the duck's tombstone. She had painted a sizable rock, found on the street, in dabs of red, white, yellow, blue and green, and written FUNNY in red topside. As she floated more flower petals over the grave, the little girl said goodbye to the duck. Her mother said, "Funny would like this place. I'm sure Funny will be happy in this garden." Funny lies very near the compost pile where, earlier in the season, I had informally recycled a ruby-crowned kinglet and two warblers that my cat, Be-bop, had downed along the Eastern Flyway, of which my garden is a very small stretch.

With the memorial service concluded, I got on with the planting: two houttuynias, a *Phuopsis stylosa,* a *Cynoglossum nervosum,* coreopsis "Goldfink," hemerocallis "Good Fairy of Oz" and so forth, but all afternoon I kept returning to my childhood garden. Growing up in the woods across Lake Washington from Seattle, my sister, brother and I each had a vegetable and a flower garden to tend, and a surfeit of pets. My flower garden, a fairly shady place, was also the family pet cemetery.

There rested Tweetie, the canary the cat caught on the bird's solo flight through the house; Pete the hamster—instead of breeding, the night I left them together, Repeat killed Pete; three bunnies—I was a notably unsuccessful rabbit breeder—when Mopsy, my white rabbit, finally gave birth, she also committed infanticide; the Muscovy ducks, GusGus and Waddles, brought down by a neighbor's boxer, who later got Mammy and Pappy, the Bantam couple. Whenever a pet died I would put the body in a Sunny Jim peanut butter jar, insert a scrap of paper with the animal's name printed for posterity, and twist the lid tight, so as to preserve my pet intact, for later exhumation. I would bury the glass peanut butter coffin in my funerary flower garden and mark the spot with a small twig cross. Each turtle, hamster, guppy, canary, etc. would be sent to R.I.P. according to modified Catholic rites, based on the old Baltimore Catechism.

So Funny, the Pekin duck, lies between Thurber, the birch, and the Chinese stationary bamboo, and has made me remember that my garden has always included dead pets, and most likely always will. One way or another—even in New York City—animals find their way into my garden, I water them and they come up roses.

—from *The Wall Street Journal,* August 22, 1989

Time

BY SUSAN HILL AND RORY STUART

Perfect moments come in every garden, though more frequently in some than others. To the very active gardener they may not be of great importance and usually they will be happy accidents, lucky moments when, chancing to glance up, the gardener will see that this or that grouping of plants at the height of their flowering looks exactly right, because of the way the light falls on them.

The moment will be pleasing but fleeting and its transience of little importance when there is satisfying work to be done and the excitement of a tray of newly germinated rare plants to absorb the attention.

This gardener does not plan for perfect moments nor depend upon them for his satisfaction. When they come, often at the end of the day when he is restfully pottering about among the flower beds, he welcomes them but sees them in perspective, for his enjoyment comes all day and every day in his active life as a plant grower.

The more contemplative gardener, seeing the garden as a

whole, the design of it, and its nature as a still place of delight and refreshment, will wait and hope for the moment when it seems to achieve perfection. Awareness of when such moments are most likely helps to make them happen; they will not be entirely accidental but anticipated; everything will be planned to encourage them. This gardener will be out in the very early morning and from late afternoon, attentive to small changes in the quality of the light and the atmosphere, as well as to every nuance of the season, which combine to create perfection. Late sunlight will slant for just a few minutes on a variegated shrub placed against a dark, evergreen background; the assertive evening calling of blackbirds and the scream of swifts round and round the rooftops calms and stills as darkness gathers; pale flowers, translucent whites, pinks and chalky blues stand out in the dusk, sharp yellows and oranges are defined separately as dimmer, subtler tones retreat into the spreading shadow. Water on a pool goes dark blue and then black at one particular moment, just as the moon rides up into a clear sky. The dew rises and with it the fainter scents which have been blotted out by the heat of the day. Now, all should be quiet, still; the air is so transmissive that any sharp sound or acrid smell will startle and upset the delicate equilibrium in the garden. Conversation and even company are inappropriate. Such moments are to be enjoyed alone. They are the reasons why some people have gardens.

But if they may be planned and looked for, such moments cannot be preserved. Time will not stand still: we cannot freeze the perfect moment, we may only wait patiently for it to be repeated, and the very intensity of the pleasure such moments give comes precisely because of their transience and their fragility—time is of their very essence. If a garden could be preserved at a moment of perfection and therefore set outside of time, it would become an embalmed garden, lifeless, and pointless as silk flowers. We do not want to live in unreal places, artificially preserved in a sanitized past (even if we may enjoy a brief holiday in resorts where, we are told, time has stood still).

Gardeners celebrate the influence of time. If we have had a late cold spring followed by a desiccating drought, autumn may be the most soft and golden for years; one poor season will sooner or later be compensated for by another. If plants fall sick and fare ill one year there is always the next, when things may have put themselves right and roses be the best ever. A luxuriant June, when everything seems to flower twice as thickly for twice as long and the whole garden tumbles out in bloom together, can, in the end, sate the appetite, so that even the smell of honeysuckle begins to cloy. On hot, still, over-sweet, leafy evenings then, the gardener may long for the austerity of cold, bare boughs, white rime and the plain penitential garden fare of midwinter. We enjoy what there is, yet long for change, stillness, a rest, like that sympathetic anonymous gardener who cried, "Hooray! The first frost. The dahlias are all dead."

There is a continuity about the garden and an order of succession in the garden year which is deeply pleasing, and in one sense there are no breaks or divisions—seed time flows on to flowering time and harvest time; no sooner is one thing dying than another is coming to life. But there are seasons and they come to an end and by late October the growing season is over. Bonfires celebrate and mark a conclusion. And once, that was that, just as it was for the farmer. After harvest, the land was ploughed and then lay fallow, resting until seed time the following spring. Now, the land is under crop the whole year round—combine harvesters one day give way to the plough the next and the seed drill on the day after that. To many people it seems unnatural and they have the same view of things in the garden. They can do nothing to change the intensive nature of modern farming, but they can certainly arrange the garden to suit themselves. They can put it to bed. Everything is cut down, tidied up, vegetables stored, mower and tools cleaned and put away; tender plants are covered or brought into the green-house, vulnerable shrubs wrapped snuggly in shrouds of sacking or fleece. The leaves are swept up, the very last bonfire darkens at the core and crumbles to ash. A line is drawn under the garden year.

It is a bare place now, muted, green and brown and black, a space of neat shapes and clean lines, to be looked out on from the warmth and shelter of the house. There is a great feeling of resolution and satisfaction at this time, when the year in the garden can be reviewed from the armchair. The next one may be planned and looked forward to but now it is time for a rest and a natural, quiet breathing space. There is also the delight of having the garden indoors for a while, as green branches and berries come in to celebrate Christmas, and the rooms are filled with the sweet smell of forced hyacinths.

—from *Reflections from a Garden*, 1995

AUTHOR BIOGRAPHIES

ABBY ADAMS gardens in upstate New York, where she contends with all the inconveniences of a Zone 5 climate. She has published two books, *An Uncommon Scold* and *The Gardener's Gripe Book*.

ELIZABETH VON ARNIM was born in New Zealand in 1866 and went to London as a young woman to study piano. She married Count Joachim von Arnim when she was twenty-four years old, and her two books about the gardens of his estate at Nassenheide, *Elizabeth and Her German Garden* and *The Solitary Summer*, became instant classics.

JANICE EMILY BOWERS is a professional botanist who lives and gardens in southern Arizona.

GEOFFREY B. CHARLESWORTH is an Englishman living in Massachusetts with a particular interest in rock gardening. A retired mathematics professor, he is the author of *The Opinionated Gardener* and *A Gardener Obsessed*, winner of the 1996 Quill & Trowel Award.

THOMAS C. COOPER is the editor of *Horticulture* magazine and the author of *Odd Lots*.

THALASSA CRUSO, once dubbed "the first lady of house-plants," was the star of the popular PBS series *Making Things Grow*. An Englishwoman who came to America in 1935, she wrote a gardening column for *The Boston Globe* for many years. Her books include *Making Things Grow* and *To Everything There Is a Season*.

ROBERT DASH is an artist and the creator of Madoo, an extraordinary garden in Sagaponak, Long Island, which is open to the public. For several years, he has contributed an occasional gardening column to *The East Hampton Star*.

PAULA DEITZ is the editor of *The Hudson Review* and writes frequently about landscape design.

EMILY DICKINSON, a nineteenth-century poet, was born and lived all her life in Amherst, Massachusetts, spending much of her adult life as a semi-recluse. Although only seven of her more than two thousand poems were published during her lifetime, she is now considered, along with Walt Whitman, to be one of the greatest American poets.

HELEN DILLON is a garden writer and lecturer who lives in Dublin, Ireland, where she is the gardening columnist for Ireland's *Sunday Tribune*.

AUSTIN DOBSON, who died in 1921, was an English civil servant all his life. He was also a poet, critic, translator, and an accomplished practitioner of light verse and parodies.

KEN DRUSE is an author and photographer who lives and gardens in Brooklyn, New York. He is a proponent of the natural gardening movement and contributes to many garden publications. His several books include *The Collector's Garden* and *The Natural Shade Garden*.

JOE ECK and WAYNE WINTERROWD are partners in a landscape and garden design firm. They live and garden at North Hill in Vermont and are frequent contributors to *Horticulture* magazine.

REGINALD FARRER was an English botanist and plant hunter who made many botanical expeditions to China, Japan, Burma, and the European Alps at the beginning of this century and wrote many books about his travels. The book he is most remembered for is *My Rock Garden*, which was published in 1907 and remained in print for more than forty years.

M.F.K. FISHER was born in California in 1908 and lived for many years in France, where she developed a lifelong passion for the art of good eating. She was the author of sixteen volumes of essays and reminiscences and the translator of Brillat-Savarin's *The Physiology of Taste*.

ROBIN LANE FOX is a professor of Greek and Roman history at Oxford, where he is also the garden master of New College. He writes weekly gardening column for the *Financial Times* and is the author of *Variations on a Garden* and *Better Gardening*.

PATTI HAGAN has been the *Wall Street Journal*'s gardening columnist since 1986; her ability to take on controversial issues has earned her the informal title of "investigative gardening columnist." She lives and gardens in Brooklyn, New York.

SUSAN HILL is a novelist who has also written two autobiographical books and several books for children. She lives and gardens in the English Cotswolds.

CAROL BISHOP HIPPS is a garden writer and photographer who lives in Huntsville, Alabama.

SAMUEL REYNOLDS HOLE was a nineteenth-century cleric and an ardent rosarian who organized the first National Rose Show in 1858. For many years the dean of Rochester, he viewed gardening as "character reform." His *A Book About Roses*, ran to more than twenty editions.

GERTRUDE JEKYLL, who died in 1932 at the age of eighty-nine, is generally acknowledged to be the first lady of modern garden design. An artist whose failing eyesight led her to take up gardening in her forties, she designed more than three hundred gardens, many of them for houses designed by her great friend Sir Edwin Lutyens. Her influence has been profound and lasting.

JAMAICA KINCAID was born on the island of St. Johns, Antigua. Her books, including her most recent publication, *The Au-*

tobiography of My Mother (1997), have received great critical praise. She lives with her family in Vermont and in recent years has become an impassioned gardener.

CYNTHIA KLING is a contributing editor of *Harper's Bazaar*.

JOSEPH WOOD KRUTCH was an author, editor, and teacher. A professor at Columbia University, he was a highly regarded social and literary critic. Before he died in 1970, he retired and moved to Arizona, where he wrote several books about nature and the natural world, including *The Desert Year* and *The Measure of Man*, winner of the National Book Award.

CHARLES KURALT was a distinguished journalist and for more than thirty years the host of CBS News' *Sunday Morning*. An inveterate traveler, he logged more than a million miles in the course of his life and his work for CBS. The recipient of three Peabody Awards and thirteen Emmys for his journalism, he was also the author of six books, including his best-selling memoir, *A Life on the Road*.

STEPHEN LACEY is an English gardening writer, lecturer, and designer. He lives in Oxford and is a regular contributor to newspapers and magazines, as well as a presenter on the BBC television series *Gardener's World*.

ALLEN LACY is a professor of philosophy at Stockton State College and lives in New Jersey. He contributes to many magazines and has written several books about gardening, including *Home Ground: A Gardener's Miscellany,* and is the editor and publisher of *Homeground,* a delightfully idiosyncratic quarterly newsletter.

ELIZABETH LAWRENCE was a gifted landscape architect and writer. The author of six books, including *A Southern Garden,* published in 1942, she was a prolific contributor to numerous gardening publications. Her writings were informed and inspired by her own legendary gardens in Raleigh and Charlotte.

CHRISTOPHER LLOYD regularly contributes a gardening column to *Country Life* and is the author of a number of garden books, including *The Year at Great Dixter,* about his own garden in Sussex, which is open to the public.

MAURICE MAETERLINCK was a Belgian author, playwright, and poet who wrote in French. In 1911 he received the Nobel Prize in Literature.

KATHERINE MANSFIELD was born in New Zealand in 1888, but went to live in England, where she quickly achieved a distinguished reputation for her poetry and short stories.

ANDREW MARVELL is considered to be one of the most elegant seventeenth-century English lyric poets. He was a parliamentarian and a prolific writer of political pamphlets.

JULIAN MEAD was a novelist who lived and gardened in Danville, Virginia, until his death in 1940. In addition to *Bouquets and Bitters,* he wrote one other book about gardening, *Adam's Profession and Its Conquest by Eve.*

W. S. MERWIN, who lives in Hawaii, is the author of numerous books of poetry, the latest of which is *The Folding Cliffs.* Among his most prestigious awards are the Pulitzer, the Bollingen, and the Tanning prizes.

HENRY MITCHELL was, before his death in 1993, the garden correspondent for *The Washington Post,* where his good sense, practical advice, and gentle humor earned him an extraordinarily loyal following that extended far beyond Washington.

MARY RUSSELL MITFORD was a playwright and poet who achieved great recognition with the publication in 1832–1843 of *Our Village,* her five-volume series of sketches about the goings-on of country life.

BEVERLEY NICHOLS was a journalist, essayist, novelist, playwright, and passionate gardener. He was considered a great wit and had an enormous circle of friends. During the course of his life, he was the author of more than thirty books, five of which are about his own gardening experiences.

MIRABEL OSLER's work appears in numerous gardening magazines. Her first book, *A Gentle Plea for Chaos,* described the making of a large, rambling country garden, which she created with her husband in Shropshire. She is now the owner of a small, eccentric town garden, also in Shropshire.

RUSSELL PAGE, a self-taught landscape designer, worked all over the world. His designs had an enormous influence on twentieth-century garden planning. (A passion for water is evident in almost all his gardens, both public and private.) His book *The Education of A Gardener,* published in 1962, is considered a garden classic.

ELEANOR PERÉNYI has worked as a journalist and has written a biography of Liszt, a novel, and a memoir of her years in Hungary. She has lived and gardened in Stonington, Connecticut, for many years. Her one book on gardening, *Green Thoughts,* has become an American gardening classic.

MICHAEL POLLAN is executive editor of *Harper's* Magazine. His writing on gardens and nature has appeared in several magazines. *Second Nature,* a book about his experiences of making a garden in Connecticut, is a delightful blend of meditation, autobiography, and social history.

ALEXANDER POPE is considered the greatest English poet of the eighteenth century, and a master of verse satire. He is probably best known for his *An Essay on Man* (1734) and *The Dunciad* (1728–43).

ANNE RAVER lives in Brooklyn. Her many articles on gardening and the environment have appeared in *The New York Times* and *Newsday*.

THEODORE ROETHKE, who died in 1963, published several volumes of poetry, including *The Waking*, which was awarded the Pulitzer Prize in 1953. His father managed greenhouses in Saginaw, Michigan, for a living, and for Roethke this greenhouse world was "both heaven and hell, a kind of tropic created in the savage climate of Michigan, where austere German-Americans turned their love of order and their terrifying efficiency into something truly beautiful."

VITA SACKVILLE-WEST was a poet, a novelist, and a gardener. Her weekly gardening column, which ran for more than twenty-five years in *The Observer*, made her a household name among English gardeners, while her own garden, Sissinghurst, which she started with her husband, Harold Nicolson, in the 1930s, has achieved a mythic stature and receives more than 150,000 visitors every year.

JAMES SCHUYLER was awarded the Pulitzer Prize in 1981 for *The Morning of the Poem*. His collected poems appeared in 1993, two years after his death. He was a central figure in the celebrated New York School of Poets.

LAUREN SPRINGER is a plantswoman by profession and for pleasure. She has worked in gardens on both sides of the Atlantic, and now lives and gardens in northern Colorado, where she writes a gardening column for *The Denver Post*.

SARA STEIN is the author of several gardening books, including *My Weeds, Noah's Garden,* and *Planting Noah's Garden.* Her horticultural interests have led her to become one of the foremost proponents of ecological gardening. She lives in Pound Ridge, New York.

RORY STUART works as a garden designer, writes and lectures on gardens, and leads garden tours. His own garden is in Gloucestershire.

CELIA THAXTER lived all her life on the Isles of Shoals, off the Maine coast, where her family ran a large resort hotel. Her own garden was the inspiration for the one book she wrote. *An Island Garden,* illustrated by Childe Hassam, was published in 1894, the year she died.

HENRY DAVID THOREAU lived as a recluse in a cabin at Walden Pond from 1845 to 1847, where he planted and tended a vegetable garden. From this experience came *Walden,* one of the great books of American literature.

PATRICIA THORPE lives in upstate New York and has written four books on gardening. *Growing Pains* is her most recent publication.

EDITH WHARTON, the celebrated American novelist, won the Pulitzer Prize in 1920 for *The Age of Innocence.* She always had a great interest in architectural and landscape design and was extremely knowledgeable about garden history, particularly in connection with France, Italy, and England.

E. B. WHITE, a staff writer at *The New Yorker* for many years died in 1985. A witty observer of contemporary life, he published many essays and verses and was also the author of *Charlotte's Web* and *Stuart Little*. He lived in Maine with his wife, Katharine S. White.

KATHARINE S. WHITE was an editor at *The New Yorker* for thirty-four years. Throughout her life she was a keen gardener, and in 1958 she wrote the first of a series of fourteen garden pieces, which appeared in *The New Yorker* over the next twelve years and were later published as a book, *Onward and Upward in the Garden*.

LOUISE BEEBE WILDER was a passionate exponent of rock gardens and during the 1920s and '30s contributed a gardening column to *House and Garden*. She was the author of ten books, including *Adventures in a Suburban Garden* and *The Fragrant Path*, and was one of the most popular garden writers of her day.

RICHARDSON WRIGHT, as the editor of *House and Garden* for over forty years, was an influential figure on the garden scene in the 1930s and '40s. He was also a onetime war correspondent in Siberia and Manchuria, and a literary and drama critic.

ACKNOWLEDGMENTS

We are grateful to the following for their permission to use these excerpts:

Arcade Publishing for "Gapers and Crouchers" from *A Breath from Elsewhere,* © 1997 by Mirabel Osler, and an excerpt from *A Gentle Plea for Chaos,* © 1989 by Mirabel Osler.

George Borchardt, Inc., for the author, for "A Shape of Water," © 1997 by W. S. Merwin.

Curtis Brown, London, for excerpts from *In Your Garden* and *Even More for Your Garden,* © 1951 and 1958 by the Estate of Vita Sackville-West, and for "Thoughts on Thistles" from *Variations on a Garden,* © 1986 by Robin Lane Fox.

Robert Dash for "Summer," © 1985 by Robert Dash.

Paula Deitz for "My Mother's Garden," © 1996 by Paula Deitz.

Doubleday, a division of Bantam Doubleday Dell Publishing Group, Inc. for "Cuttings (Later)," © 1948 by Theodore Roethke from *The Collected Poems of Theodore Roethke.*

Ken Druse for permission to publish an excerpt from *The Collector's Garden,* © 1996 by Ken Druse, Clarkson N. Potter/Publishers.

Farrar, Straus & Giroux, Inc., for "Horse-Chestnut Trees and Roses" from *Collected Poems* by James Schuyler, © 1993 by the Estate of James Schuyler; "Hydrangeas? Never!" from *Home Ground: A Gardener's Miscellany,* © 1984 by Allen Lacy; and excerpts from the "Introduction" by E. B. White and "The Changing Rose, the Enduring Cabbage" from *Onward and Upward in the Garden* by Katharine S. White, © 1979 by E. B. White as Executor of the Estate of Katharine S. White. Introduction © 1979 by E. B. White.

Fulcrum Publishing for an excerpt from *The Undaunted Garden,* © 1994 by Lauren Springer.

Eric Glass Ltd., for the Estate of Beverley Nichols, for excerpts from *A Garden Open Tomorrow,* © 1968 by Beverley Nichols.

David Godine, Publisher, Inc., for excerpts from *The Opinionated Gardener,* © 1988 by Geoffrey B. Charlesworth; *A Gardener Obsessed,* © 1994 by Geoffrey B. Charlesworth; and *The Startling Jungle,* © 1986 by Stephen Lacey.

Grove Atlantic, Inc., for an excerpt from *Second Nature,* © 1991 by Michael Pollan.

Patti Hagan for "Dust to Dust," © 1989 by Patti Hagan.

Harcourt Brace & Company for an excerpt from "The Day of the Living Dead" in *Growing Pains: Time and Change in the Garden,* © 1994 by Patricia Thorpe.

Henry Holt and Company, Inc., for an excerpt from *Odd Lots: Seasonal Notes of a City Gardener,* © 1995 by Thomas C. Cooper.

Houghton Mifflin for an excerpt from *One Man's Garden*, © 1952 by Henry Mitchell.

Indiana University Press for an excerpt from *The Essential Earthman*, © 1981 by Henry Mitchell.

Melanie Jackson Agency for "My Invisible Garden" from *Deep in the Green*, © 1995 by Anne Raver.

Jamaica Kincaid for an excerpt from "A Fire by Ice," © 1993 by Jamaica Kincaid.

Cynthia Kling for *Down and Dirty*, © 1997 by Cynthia Kling.

Alfred A. Knopf, Inc., for an excerpt from *To Everything There Is a Season*, © 1971, 1972, 1973 by Thalassa Cruso.

Frances Lincoln Publishers for an excerpt from *Scent in Your Garden*, © 1991 by Stephen Lacey.

Little, Brown and Company for an excerpt from *Four Seasons in a Vermont Garden*, by Joe Eck and Wayne Winterrowd, © 1995 by Joseph Eck and Wayne Winterrowd.

Macmillan General Reference USA, a Simon & Schuster Macmillan Company, for excerpts from *Garden Artistry*, © 1995 by Helen Dillon; *In a Southern Garden*, © by Carol Bishop Hipps; and "Hurrah for Vulgarity" from *In My Garden*, © 1994 by Christopher Lloyd.

Pavilion Books for an excerpt from *Reflections from a Garden*, © 1995 by Susan Hill and Rory Stuart.

Putnam Publishing Group for an excerpt from *Charles Kuralt's America*, © 1995 by Charles Kuralt.

Random House for "Help" from *Green Thoughts*, © 1981 by Eleanor Perényi.

Rayford Clayton Reddell for permission to use the introduction by M.F.K. Fisher to *Growing Good Roses*, © 1988 by Rayford Clayton Reddell.

Trustees of Columbia University for "February" from *The Twelve Seasons*, © 1949 by Joseph Wood Krutch.

University of Arizona Press for "A Garden Like a Life" from *A Full Life in a Small Place*, © 1993 by Janice Emily Bowers.

Wallace Literary Agency, Inc., for an excerpt from *My Weeds: A Gardener's Botany*, © 1988 by Sara B. Stein.

Warren Way for "The Onset of Spring," © 1943 by Elizabeth Lawrence.

Workman Publishing Company, Inc., for an excerpt from *The Gardener's Gripe Book*, © 1995 by Abby Adams.

Special thanks to Katherine Powis, Librarian at The New York Horticultural Society, for her gracious and invaluable assistance in checking sources and locating hard to find material.

A NOTE ON THE TYPE

This book was set in Fournier, a typeface named for Pierre Simon Fournier *fils* (1712–1768), a celebrated French type designer. Coming from a family of typefounders, Fournier was an extraordinarily prolific designer of typefaces and of typographic ornaments. He was also the author of the important *Manuel typographique* (1764–1766), in which he attempted to work out a system standardizing type measurement in points, a system that is still in use internationally. In 1925 Fournier type was revived by the Monotype Corporation of London.

The display type of this book was set in Eden light.